EIGHT DAVE'S ARE WEAK

Eight Dave's Are Weak

Byron James-Adams

Eight Dave's Are Weak
Copyright @ 2025 James Byron Books
www.jamesbyronbooks.com

All rights reserved. No part of this publication may be reproduced, distributed, or transmitted in any form or by any means, including photocopying, recording, or other electronic or mechanical methods, without the prior written permission of the author, except in the case of brief quotations embodied in critical reviews and certain other non-commercial uses permitted by copyright law.

This story is fictitious. Some long-standing institutions, agencies, and public offices do exist. The characters and situations involved are wholly imaginary, and resemblance to natural persons, living or dead, or actual events is purely coincidental. Please accept any errors, omissions and oversights as this book has not been produced with the assistance of A.I.

Again thanks to my beta readers. Vic, Lil & R.F.A.

Cover Art: Canva by author.
Internal Book Design: Ingram Sparks.

2 – BYRON JAMES-ADAMS

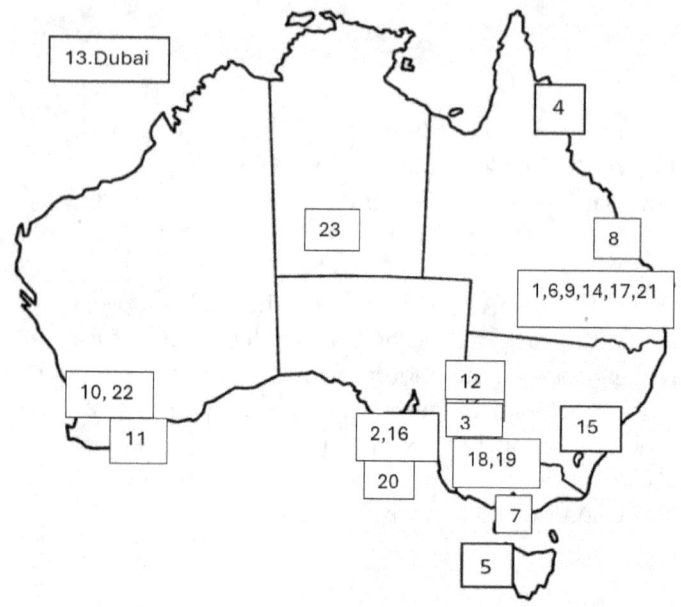

One Tricked Phoney:
Brisbane 1, Adelaide 2, Pinnaroo 3.
Two Hurtled Gloves:
Port Douglas 4, Corrina 5, Brisbane 6.
Three French Bens:
Melbourne 7, Rockhampton 8, Brisbane 9.
Four Brooding Birds:
Busselton 10, Margaret River 11, Broken Hill 12
Five Mouldy Bins:
Dubai 13, Brisbane 14, Sydney 15
Six Geezers Lying: Adelaide 16, Brisbane 17
Seven Hapless Hoops:
Ouyen 18, Mildura 19, Kangaroo Island 20
Eight Dave's Are Weak:
Brisbane 21, Perth 22, Alice Springs 23

1

Rosemary Palmer was surrounded by stuff, but it wasn't the good stuff between chocolate macaroon cupcakes, it was the stuff you find in the remnants of dead computers. Rose picked up a motherboard and tossed it into the box labelled "Motherboards," however, the next piece of hardware was a little more challenging, as it was a tiny flat plastic box with protruding wires. It looked like a dead centipede.

Rose referred to the list she had been provided, where each piece had been hand-drawn and labelled accordingly, and considered where to put it. Nic Thorn, Rose's friend, mentor, and scam-busting associate, entered the room holding another box of the crunchy, crushed computer bits and dropped it on the table.

'What have you found?'

Rose picked up the crushed piece of computer candy and was about to suggest where he could put the next box when her phone rang.

Swiping upwards, there was silence at the other end of the telephone, so she re-read the number and confirmed it was her mother, Jana, calling and she began to hyperventilate between loud sobs: 'They've taken your Father off to jail. He's been arrested for his involvement in a cryptocurrency fraud. Whatever that means.'

Nic overheard the comment and moved closer so then Rose used her finger to cover the mouthpiece: 'Apparently, my Father has been taken off to jail.' Rose finally broke into the conversation. 'It will work out, whatever it is, Mother, as long as no one has died. Has someone died?'

Jana then took a loud gulp of air. 'No Rosemary, but that's not the point.'

Rose sighed, then added. 'Unless *he* killed someone, and I haven't heard anything regarding that.' Jana slowed down. 'No, he hasn't, he didn't, but he's...they came and took him away. He was handcuffed, and the whole street watched as they put him into the backseat of the Police Car. It was so embarrassing.'

'What time was this?'

'About three this afternoon. It was right in the middle of the school run. Everyone stopped to see what was going on. I rang Mr Wonderful, Michael. He said not to worry about it.'

Rose sighed heavily this time at the mention of her ex-husband: - Rose was required to marry

Michael due to a stern directive from her father to win over a business deal. The marriage lasted three very long days, and the business deal didn't last much longer. Although over ten years ago, Rose still struggles to come to terms with it.

'Mother, please stop calling him that. Was Michael arrested too?'

Jana took a breath. 'No, Rosemary. Why would you expect that? He's a wonderful man, and I hope one day you'll see what you missed out on by not staying married to him.'

Rose did a mental head-slap. 'What did Michael tell you? Is he going to the Police Station to talk to them?'

'No, not at all. Why would he be doing that?'

'You said Father had been arrested for fraud, Michael is his Accountant.'

Jana sighed. 'Well, when I talked to Michael, he said he was too busy to talk about it. I also had a call from Davide Reed, the Managing Partner at Michael's firm. Davide told me he was also looking for Michael. They don't know where he is.'

Rose shook her head and whispered to Nic. 'I bet he's busy shredding evidence.' Jana had overheard. 'What's that you said, Rosemary?'

'Nothing, Mother. Please leave it with me, and I'll call you back.'

'What can you do, Rosemary? And besides, where are you this time?'

'I'm here in Brisbane, working on another fraud investigation with Nic.'

Jana harrumphed. 'Isn't it time you stopped wasting time with that man and got a real job? Besides, I didn't expect you to be able to do anything about it. I rang in case you wanted to know.' Jana then disconnected without saying goodbye.

Rose looked at Nic. 'I guess we should call Chewy. He can do his computer thing finding out about things.'

Chewy was their scam-busting associate and go-to computer guy, and while he is based in West Brunswick, Melbourne, he had his finger on the pulse for any background searches of stuff and provided support for their investigations.

Nic nodded. 'Yep, and I've already sent a text to my contact with Queensland Police. She'll call me back in a tick.' Rose called Chewy but he was busy servicing his Falcon, so left a message for him to try and find Michael.

The duo continued to catalogue the computer candy when Nic's phone rang. He stepped away to take the call, then returned to Rose. 'That was Angie, my contact in the Fraud Squad. She confirmed your Father has been implicated in a multi-million dollar crypto fraud and is facing up to ten years in jail. She also mentioned he won't get out of custody unless he can post bail of half a million dollars.'

Rose sighed. 'What about Michael? Has he been arrested too?'

'Not yet, as they can't find him.'

'Does my Mother know about the bail?'

Nic shook his head. 'I assume not yet. Can she ante up that sort of coin?' Rose continued. 'I would suspect so. Their property at Hamilton is worth about seven million, and the last time I saw the Family Trust Accounts, they held over ten million in assets.'

'Wow, I might have to stop paying you.'

'You don't pay me anything now.'

'There is that. Anyway, we'll try Dimond, to see if she knows where he is. Angie also said they don't want to go to the expense of issuing an arrest warrant for him at this stage, as it might complicate things.'

Rose reluctantly called Dimond, and knew it would be a drama as she didn't enjoy listening to the ramblings of her ex-husband's wife. The call was answered as soon as it rang: 'This is Dimond.'

'Hi Dimond, it's Rose. Have you heard anything from Michael regarding my Father being arrested for fraud?'

'No, I haven't. I haven't seen Michael for over a week. I think he's on a holiday somewhere. He never tells me anything.'

'When was the last time you spoke to him?'

'Do you mean before he left?'

'Yes. Does that mean you don't speak to him when he's at home?'

'Not really. I hardly see him since we moved into our new home at Brookwater Estate. It's huge. He hides in his little den or on the golf course. They have bunkers taller than he is.'

Rose subconsciously nodded her head in agreement. 'Anyway, what about Lucy and Skye? Does he speak to them?'

'No, our little darling daughters are boarding at Sommerville College in Brisbane, so I'm rattling around in The Great White House all alone.'

Rose momentarily parked the name that Dimond had called her new abode and continued: 'Why do you send the girls to boarding school? There must be one closer, besides Brookwater is on the Ipswich train line. They could catch a train to school.' Dimond sighed. 'It's a long story. Michael thought it would be good for their education and ideal for us to get closer, if the girls were in a boarding school, but he's never home.'

Rose shook her head. 'OK. I don't want to know anything about what you two get up to. My Father has been arrested on cryptocurrency laundering and fraud charges, and as Michael is his Accountant, He would know what's happening.'

Dimond went quiet for a moment. 'That might explain the postcard I've just received.'

Rose held the phone out from her ear and shook her head in frustration. 'I thought you didn't know where he was.' Dimond paused again. 'I know where he was, just not where he is. It was dated last Tuesday. I have no idea what day it is.'

Rose realised the conversation wasn't going anywhere and decided to close the call. 'I have to go, Dimond. I'll call you if something comes up, or when you hear from Michael, please let me know.' Dimond stammered with her response. 'Why would he ring me? I have no idea how his mind works.'

'Goodbye Dimond.' Rose disconnected. 'What a waste of time.'

Nic nodded. 'Are you referring to the call, Dimond or Michael?'

'All of them.'

Rose's phone rang again but she didn't recognise the number: 'This is Rose.'

'Well, fancy that...you took my call.'

Rose switched her phone to the speaker and beckoned Nic to come closer. 'Just what have you got my Father involved in Michael, and where are you?'

The call was disconnected, and a few moments later, Nic's phone rang. 'Hey Chewy. Did you find Michael?' Chewy laughed. 'Yes, he's using a burner phone, but the dope forgot to turn off his other one, so I rang his number and he answered. I told him he'd won a million dollars in a South African lottery, and almost burst out laughing when he started to give me his Bank details and logon passwords so I could send the money to his bank account.'

Nic grinned. 'So, where is he?'

'At an address in Browns Plains, south of Brisbane. I googled the place and searched for the property ownership. It turns out Matt Seaford owns it. He's the guy we busted a couple of years ago for the bogus banking scam.'

Rose overheard the name. 'Is Matt Seaford out of jail already?'

Chewy responded. 'Nope. He purchased the property before starting his downward spiral into his little banking scam, and as it wasn't purchased with the proceeds of his crimes, he can legally retain it. There's still a small mortgage on it, and it's currently tenanted.'

'Is Michael renting it?'

'I don't think so. He could just be hiding out there.'

Nic nodded again. 'I'll have someone masquerading as a representative from the Fraud Squad to visit him. Can you give him a call-back?'

'Sure. Who are you thinking of using?'

Nic looked at Rose. 'I know a few people that would be happy to do it.'

Rose grinned. 'I would, and I'll even put on disguise to scare him.' Nic continued. 'I'll call Angie to see if we can get an arrest warrant or at least a "Go directly to jail card without collecting $200."

Nic moved away, made the call, and returned moments later: 'They won't issue an arrest warrant out for him as they haven't worked out the link between him or his firm and the money laundering thing your Father is involved in. They are still working on putting the jigsaw together. We might be on our own with this one.' Rose nodded. 'So, are we heading down to Browns Plains?'

'Nup. I'll call Chewy back, and he can do his thing to clone Michael's phone so we can keep tabs on him. I'd have to assume he'd be using his normal phone to call Dimond, and that's why it's still turned on.'

Nic called Chewy, and they were able to listen into a conversation he was having with Dimond. Michael was his usual condescending self: 'Oh, Di, don't cry or be angry or be anything. I'll be back home soon. I'm in Bali and booked on the next flight home.' Dimond went silent. 'Are you still there, Dimond?'

'Yes, but you can't be in Bali, as there's a cyclone there now. I'm watching it on your stupid hundred-and-fifty-centimetre television. What's going on Michael?'

'Nothing you have to worry about. Go and get your nails or hair done and tell the girls I'll see them when I see them.'

Dimond hesitated again. 'When do I tell them you'll be home?' Michael responded quickly 'Later, Di. Just deal with it. I have to go, and if Rose, and her sidekick Nic The Private Dick, ask about me, you've not heard anything.' Dimond sighed heavily. 'Is there anything else you want to tell me? Do you still love me, Michael?' Michael grunted and abruptly disconnected.

Rose leaned back from the call and shook her head. 'Now he's even lying to Dimond.' Nic grinned. 'At least we can keep tabs on him as long as he doesn't turn his phone off, but I don't think he'll do anything stupid. Maybe I should clarify that: something no stupider than he's done before.'

Rose sighed. 'Stupider is not even a word.'

Nic nodded. 'Well, 'Something Stupider' is a great song. Robbie Williams and Nicole Kidman did a version on one of his early albums.' Nic broke into the song and Rose shook her head.

'Please stop singing, we've got work to do. Anyway, the song is called 'Something Stupid', not stupider. Frank and Nancy Sinatra did a version in '67, but the original was done by Carson Parkes and his wife, Gaile, a year earlier.'

Nic grinned at her knowledge of music trivia then called Chewy 'Can you call Michael to see if he'll provide his Credit Card number to you. We'll report it stolen, which might get him arrested if he tries to use it.'

Rose looked at Nic. 'How does that work? Surely someone can't ring the bank and say someone else's card is stolen? What about all of their security questions or the logon PIN?'

'If you find a Credit Card on the street and call the Bank, they will put a stop on it until it is returned to a local branch.'

Rose hesitated. 'That makes sense, but to pretend you're someone else to fool a Bank is something entirely different.'

Nic continued: 'Well, it depends on whether you have updated the voice security protocols with them. You could contact the Bank and pretend you are Dimond. If it's a joint account and she's lost her card, they would cancel his card too.'

Rose shook her head. 'I don't think I'm up to doing that.'

'Just an option. Chewy will take care of it.'

Rose looked at him. 'Just how often do you pretend you're someone else?'

Nic smiled. 'Was that a rhetorical question?'

2

The following day, they were back in the office working through the bibs, bobs and bashed binary bits when Rose's phone rang, and her demeanour changed upon taking the call: 'Yes, Sir, understood. We'll be there within the hour.' Rose disconnected. 'Well, that was interesting as we've been summoned to the Police Headquarters in Roma Street to discuss my Father's situation. That was the secretary to the Police Commissioner.'

Nic and Rose changed into attire befitting a formal visit to the Police Headquarters and were driving along Ann Street looking for a park. Rose took the opportunity to ring her Mother for an update and set the phone to speaker: 'Mother, it's me. Any news on Father?'

'No, and I'm getting quite anxious about it.'

'OK, we'll see what we can do from here. Nic has a contact in the Fraud Squad, so we'll get an update.'

Jana scoffed at the comment. 'I suspect he would. Michael has told me that Nic has been arrested so many times.'

Nic responded. 'Technically, I've never been arrested, and in case it's needed, one of my direct line of contacts is Penelope Anderson, the Deputy Commissioner of Police, here in Brisbane.'

Jana again scoffed at Nic's comment. 'I don't think so. Michael told me you would try something like this, and name-dropping doesn't mean anything to me.'

Rose shook her head in dismay, knowing that her Mother was always one to drop the name of the latest whomever she'd met at the Tattersall's Club in Brisbane or at one of her famous garden parties. 'When did you speak to Michael?'

'He visited me this morning, which is more than you have done. Anyway, we had a lovely chat over a cup of tea, and he told me everything would be OK.'

Rose shook her head again. 'He's hiding from the Police, Mother. I spoke to Dimond yesterday, and he told her he was in Bali, but we've discovered he's here in Brisbane, staying at a house in Browns Plains.'

'I don't want to hear this, Rosemary. Michael told me he would sort it all out.'

Jana hung up, and Rose sighed, then felt a tear welling only to dismissively wipe it away. 'I wonder if the day is going to get any better.'

Nic smiled. 'It just did. I found a car park on the street. How good is that?'

Nic and Rose were waiting in the foyer to be escorted to their meeting, and a Duty Sergeant led them to a conference room. They entered, and Rose noticed one entire wall comprised of a large television screen. A Cisco Communication console was in the middle of the table, and a mirrored interior window was on the opposite side of the room. The room, however, was otherwise empty.

The Duty Sergeant left, the television screen flickered, and a face appeared. It was Chewy, and Rose recognised the layout behind him. He was sitting in the basement of his house. It was wall-to-wall computer screens and other geeky stuff. Rose waved at him. 'I didn't realise you were summoned too.'

'We are being brought in to investigate a major cryptocurrency scam. It's based in Brisbane, but appears to have its tentacles all over Australia.'

Rose looked over to Nic. 'And I assume that involves my Father?'

Nic nodded. 'Yep, and mine.' Rose was surprised at his response as Nic had a policy that his family was never involved in anything they investigated.

They sat there waiting for something to start when a voice broke the silence via the intercom: 'Thank you for coming in at such short notice. Hello Chewy, you look well.' Chewy mock-saluted, and Rose whispered to Nic. 'Who is the person speaking?'

Nic returned the whisper. 'My Father.'

Rose looked at the interior window. 'Is he watching us from behind the glass? I want to meet him.'

'You could, but I don't know where he is or what he looks like.'

The voice continued: 'As you know, Rose's Father was being held pending the finalisation of bail conditions, but I've taken care of that. He will be released and you are authorised to collect and return him home, although his passport will need to be surrendered.'

Rose leaned towards the console. 'Have you spoken to Jana...my Mother? The voice responded. 'No, sorry, Rose. I'm not permitted to talk to her as it may compromise the investigation.'

Rose nodded. 'Did they raise the bail money?'

Nic put his hand on Rose's arm. 'They didn't have to.' The voice continued: 'I've arranged for you to consult with the Australian Federal Police and be part of the Task Force looking into this matter. There will be an update at two o'clock on Wednesday, in three days. It should be enough time for your team to commence your investigation.'

Nic nodded. 'That's correct, Sir.'

'Good. Keep me informed on the progress, check your schedules, and confirm your availability. Sandy Fraser will not need to return from Adelaide to help you at this stage.'

Rose whispered to Nic, after hearing the reference to her BFF, Sandy. 'Is there anything or anyone he doesn't know?'

Nic smiled. 'He hasn't met your ten-kilogram Maine Coon cat, Dog.' There was a momentary pause from the speaker. 'It's 14:15, at the moment. I'll expect an update by the close of the day.'

Nic nodded again. 'Thank you, Sir.'

The voice terminated the call and Rose smiled. 'So, you do work for your Father.'

Nic shrugged, however, Chewy responded: 'Not specifically. We get called in to find stuff, look at stuff, and do stuff. In this case, we're dealing with some real Police stuff, not unlike the fraud and scamming stuff we usually investigate.'

Rose suddenly realised that Nic's Father may have been in the adjacent room, so she stood up quickly and moved towards the door. 'I'm going to meet him. I missed him in Canberra when we did that leasing thing, so here's my chance.'

Nic waved as Rose stood up. 'Say hello for me when you do.'

Rose opened the door, stepped into the next room, and was surprised that a man was sitting there. He stood up and held out his hand. 'Please, take a seat.' The man sat down and Rose realised that she'd turned left instead of right when exiting the other room. 'I'm sorry, I believe I'm in the wrong room.'

The man nodded. 'I thought you might be.' Rose quickly exited, moved across to the other side, and opened the door, but the room was empty. 'Damn you, Nic.'

The Duty Sargeant was walking past. 'Are you looking for Mr Thorn Senior? He's just left. You might catch him in the foyer.' Rose shrugged. 'But I don't know what he looks like.' The man nodded. 'He is wearing a grey suit and carrying a black umbrella.'

Rose hurried to the foyer and looked around. It had just started raining; the fat, blobby rain that Brisbanites have to put up with during the humid summers, so the hall was now full of grey suits and black umbrellas. Rose sighed and waited a few minutes before returning to the conference room where Nic was still conversing with Chewy. There were two Styrofoam cups on the table.

Rose sat down, noticed one was empty, and picked up the other. It, too, was empty. 'I missed him.'

Nic nodded. 'If only you'd waited. I just had a coffee with him. We wondered where you went and why you didn't come back to meet him.'

'Double Damn, you Nic Thorn, Thorn.'

Nic shrugged. 'Chewy will put a brief together by the end of the day, and, as your father is scheduled to appear before a magistrate to be formally charged tomorrow, we can collect now and take him home.'

Nic saluted at the television screen. 'Catch you round like a BB8 android, Chewy.'

The television screen then went blank so Nic collected the coffee cups, broke them up, and dropped them into three different rubbish bins on the way out of the building. 'You know you could get my Father's DNA from these coffee cups.'

Rose held out a pen and pointed it at Nic. 'And I could get his DNA from you with a single jab from this pen.'

The Duty Sargeant returned and they were led to the holding cells to collect Rose's Father. The Watchhouse Officer looked at the paperwork. 'You must have friends in high places, sir, this is the quickest release I've ever seen.' Rose's father glared at him. 'Don't you know who I am?'

The Officer returned the stare and then looked down at the paperwork. 'It says here that you are Zachariah Emmerson Palmer, if that's not the case please step back inside and deal with you later.'

Rose put her hand on her Father's arm. 'Come on, Father let's go home.'

As they arrived Jana stormed out from the front gate. 'Do you know what has happened? It's an absolute disaster.' Rose looked at her. 'We've collected Father and brought him home, so where's the disaster?'

Jana sighed heavily. 'Mr and Mrs Croud, our housekeepers have left. It's an absolute disaster. They've walked out and left me to deal with everything.'

Nic smiled and whispered to Rose. 'It's all your fault, you know.'

Rose offered to assist her father from the car, but he waved her away dismissively and he quickly moved towards Jana. 'How could you let this happen, Jana. How could you?'

Rose moved closer to Nic as they watched as Zachariah and Jana scurried back into the house. Rose turned to face Nic. 'And this is my fault. How?'

'Well, I seem to recall that a couple of years ago, you mentioned to John and Julia that Australia is a big country, and they should get out and see it instead of staying in Brisbane working for your parents.'

'I never said that.'

'Maybe you didn't, but they did contact me recently for advice to cash out some of their investments. I put them onto a Financial Advisor and boom, they're off like a bucket of prawns in the hot sun.'

Rose sighed. 'So, it's your fault then.'

'Nup, it's the chicken and egg thing. You planted the idea, whereas I just helped them with how to lay it.'

Rose shrugged, then looked up at her parent's sprawling Hamilton house. 'I guess they're not expecting us to follow them in.'

3

About twenty minutes later, Nic and Rose were back at his warehouse still sorting the myriad of crushed computer candy. Nic picked up another motherboard. 'I'm getting a bit sick of this, but we've got at least another day of work to sort through it all.' Rose nodded. 'Wait. What about my Father's court appearance? It's scheduled for two tomorrow, and we need to submit the brief to your Father.'

'That's been taken care of. It is best to leave it for the silks and wiggy people who know how to speak silky and wiggy. Your Father will make a plea and be released on his recognisance. Any more questions?'

Rose sighed. 'Oh yes, I have many more, like who wrote the book on men.'

Nic smiled. 'Well, it wasn't me, but I can tell you once we've sorted all of this stuff out, we can start on the really boring stuff.'

Rose stopped mid-throw. 'More boring than this? Why have we been sorting through all this stuff for the last couple of days? What are we looking for?'

Nic shrugged 'I think it's something to do with investigating a cryptocurrency fraud.' He then placed his hand on a folder on the table. 'But the good news is we have another investigation. We're heading off to the MacDonnell Ranges to find some gold. It's west of Alice Springs, near the Western Australian border.'

Nic broke into the late 70's song by John Stewart. "Turning Music into Gold,' but he had changed the word music in the title to gold and sang 'Turning gold into gold.'

Rose shook her head. 'Nic, please don't mess with the words you have a hard enough time using them in speech. What's the latest with my Father?'

'It's been taken care of and will stay out of the news until we sort out this gold thing. His next hearing will be in about two months, which will be enough time to investigate our new investigation and solve the old crypto investigation.'

Rose nodded. 'So, is that why we've been dealing with all this candy crush computer stuff?' Nic smiled. 'Boy, you ask a lot of questions. It won't go anywhere while we're away.' Nic then leaned forward, handed over another dossier, and opened his copy. 'Have you heard of Lassiter's Reef?'

Rose nodded. 'It was something about someone who found something that turned out to be nothing. It's an Australian legend that started about a hundred years ago. The guy reckons there is an untapped vein of gold somewhere out that way.'

Nic nodded. 'Yep, and the gist of our investigation is that there is truly gold in them thar hills.' Nic began to stretch and his phone rang. 'Yep, good. Thanks.' Nic closed the call and Rose looked at him. 'So what was that all about?' Nic smiled. 'We're off to Perth.'

The following morning Nic was assisting Rose put her luggage into an Uber. Rose began to secure her QANTAS flight tags and Nic put his hand out to stop her. 'We're not flying, so you can leave those tags behind.' Rose looked at him. 'You said we were going to Perth, and it's about a four thousand kilometre drive, and takes around fifty hours if you don't stop to look at the brown, flat, dry boring scenery along the way. Mighty expensive Uber trip.'

Nic smiled. 'Yep, but I did say we're off to Perth. We're heading to the Brisbane Cruise Ship Terminal and are due to board in an hour. Didn't you read the brief?'

Rose shrugged. 'I was waiting until we boarded the plane. I'll have plenty of time now though, as a cruise from Brisbane to Perth takes six or seven days if you don't stop to look at the blue, flat, wet, boring scenery along the way.'

They were dropped at the terminal and Nic handed Rose an envelope. 'This is the new brief. Forget all you know about the old brief.' Rose looked around for a seat, but decided to sit on her luggage. The review contained a few lines and two small photographs: One of a woman in her early fifties with jet-black hair and matching jet-black reading glasses. The other, late thirties with red hair and freckles. Both of them looked harmless, making Rose wonder how they were linked to the investigation:

Your name is Rosalinda Jardin. You will be on your own. Ignore me and whatever I am doing. Seek out these two women: Davida Goldsworthy (black hair) and Amethyst Davey (strawberry blonde). You should find them in the casino. Make their acquaintance. Gamble heavily. You are recently divorced. Your husband sold his Dot.Com business for millions. You may not see me on the cruise as I will be invisible. Find me in Perth.

Rose re-read her pseudonym for the investigation. "Rosalinda Jardin" which could loosely be translated in French to "Rose Garden," then she handed the note and photos back to Nic. 'Damn you, Nic. I thought you'd run out of Rose jokes.'

Nic shrugged and then extracted a light blue "Tiffany" case from his pocket.

Rose undid the bow and opened it - inside was a black pearl necklace with matching earrings, and a small earbud. 'Noice.'

Nic waited while Rose put in the earbud. 'The earbud will let you hear what I'm up to. It will be connected to the ship's wi-fi once we board, so the signal will stay strong no matter what.'

Rose settled the earpiece in her ear. 'The mind boggles.' Nic continued: 'You'll be able to talk to me via the watch, but only if I have my function set to receive and transmit. Oh, and it will start chirping if I'm getting close to you.' Nic held his wrist to his mouth. 'Testing, one-two-three.'

Rose tapped at her ear. ' Loud and clear', then she carefully placed the necklace over her head and closed the clasp. 'Is it really from Tiffany?'

Nic smiled. 'And worth about thirty grand, so try not to lose it. Other than that you're ready to go.' Rose pulled at the necklace to ensure it was secure, and nodded.

Nic and Rose then attached their cabin labels to their cases and followed the crowd toward the cruise reception area to drop off their luggage. Rose was called forward to be processed and noticed Nic had moved away. The hostess looked for him. 'Aren't you two travelling together?'

Rose responded quickly. 'Together with who?'

'The man that you arrived with. I was people-watching and noticed that you'd arrived together.' Rose shook her head. 'No, he was just walking with me. We came from the Westin Hotel and shared the Uber from the city. He overheard that I was coming here. I don't know anything about him. He didn't even offer to pay.'

The hostess grinned, then handed Rose the on-board pass card. 'You're in one of our premium suites. It's quite a large cabin just for one person. It has a wrap-around balcony, and is very private.' Rose nodded and the hostess continued: 'First time cruising with us?'

Rose smiled. 'It's actually my first cruise since losing my husband.'

The hostess leaned forward and returned the smile. 'Sorry to hear about your husband. There are often other passengers recently widowed so you might find a new husband on board.'

'Oh, no he's still pretty much alive. I divorced him after he got caught with his um ...and his secretary, you know the old cliche. He had to sell his Dot.Com business and I got half the proceeds.' Rose then checked the pass card and noticed it only showed "V.I.P.," and her suite number.

The hostess nodded. 'Welcome aboard, Ms Jardin. Just follow the crowd, then head for the lounge bar on Level 9 to complete your Safety Briefing. You'll find cocktails are being served, and while that happens, your luggage will be delivered to your room.'

Rose placed the card in her pocket. 'Thank you. I'm looking forward to it.'

4

Rose was sitting in the lounge bar on Level 9 sipping on a Singapore Sling mocktail when there was a loud commotion as a group of men had entered, followed by a gaggle of women. They were all laughing and yelling, and Nic was at the front of the group. He raised his hand to the barman. 'Drinks are on me. Room um...I can't remember what cabin I'm in.'

Nic then looked at the entourage. 'Would any of you ladies like to guess which room I'm in? Or maybe I could guess which rooms that you're in?' A couple of the women giggled and a couple of the men goggled.

Rose finished the drink, thanked the barman, and headed off to her suite. It was at least a two-minute walk from the Level 9 bar. Rose opened the door, took a moment to familiarise herself with the surroundings and assumed her suitcase hadn't been delivered, so she entered the Master Bedroom and noticed the door leading to a spacious ensuite on the opposite side. There was a generous row of wardrobes so she opened the nearest one, saw her suitcases were inside. Her clothes were already hung up, and shoes stored.

Rose closed the doors, then realised the wardrobe included additional clothes, so reopened the door and recognised they were from the recently released Carla Zampatti summer line. Rose returned to the living area, sat down on the Chesterfield leather three-seater, and considered what to do next.

A preview of the Duty-Free on-board shops was not an option as the ship was still in port, so she decided to call her BFF, Sandy who was currently in Adelaide. 'Hey, how's it going? How's your Father?' Sandy sighed. 'I think the whole of Adelaide got through this COVID thing fairly unscathed. They shut down the city, shops, and everything. I'm staying down here for another month or so. How is Dog?'

'He's fine. Behaving like any ten-kilogram cat would, eating everyone out of house and home. Dave, our friendly neighbourhood neighbour is again looking after him. We must do something to thank him for all his help when this is all over. Nic and I are heading to Perth for another investigation. It has something to do with gold. I haven't had a chance to find out everything as yet, but have the next few days to do so before we arrive.'

'Where are you?'

'In Brisbane, at the Pinkenba Cruise Terminal. I'm sitting in a cabin on board the Sea Princess in one of The Mansion Suites. It looks around one twenty metre square and comes with a massive bedroom and lounge area and uninterrupted balcony views from the aft. The ship sails in about ten minutes.'

Sandy went a little quiet. 'Is Nic there with you?'

Rose sighed. 'No, I have no idea where he is. He's on board somewhere, but I've been instructed to ignore him.'

Sandy responded quickly. 'What else do you have to do?'

'Go to the casino and meet some poker players. I've got some serious learning as I guess I need to know what I am doing. The only time I've played was with you, and we used a jar of olives whilst downing martinis. It got a bit messy.'

Sandy laughed. 'Well, nothing much is happening down here. I'll be here for a while, playing nurse for Dad. Oh, and I'm really sorry, I'll miss your big birthday tomorrow. The Big Three-Oh, I hope you get to celebrate it.'

Rose smiled. 'I'll send you some cake. I've just heard three blasts so we must be leaving port. I'm not sure about phone reception while we're at sea.'

Sandy responded. 'OK, and remember to stay away from Nic, even if you can't see him.'

EIGHT DAVE'S ARE WEAK − 33

They both laughed, but just before disconnecting Sandy called out: 'Oh, and I hope you like your new couture. Happy birthday.'

Rose located the television remote and scrolled through to find a channel dedicated to the on-board casino. It went through the gaming options introducing the slot machines and the tables which included Three-Card Poker, Texas Hold 'em, craps, and roulette. Rose decided to focus on Texas Hold 'em and began reading through the rules: *Players seek to have the best five-card poker hand from any combination of the seven cards: the five dealer cards and their two cards. The betting options are either check, call, raise, or fold. Rounds of betting take place before the flop is dealt with and after each deal.* Rose reviewed the instructions and the programme showed a real game. One of the players was the late, Shane Warne, who had become a champion poker player when he retired from cricket, and the commentator began to point out each of the players "Tells."

Rose took a pad from the escritoire and wrote down some of the indicators, along with the card-playing terms. Once the game finished, the commentator critiqued his observations against the betting processes, and at least eighty percent of the time, his predictions were correct.

Rose smiled at the outcome: 'Poker is all about playing the player, not the game. I'll need to practice my poker face.'

Rose turned off the television, recalled the names of the two women she was to meet and stepped out onto the balcony to take in the sea air, and overheard a man's voice coming from the adjacent balcony. He sounded annoyed. 'Why can't I smoke? Why can't we go to the casino? Why can't we get room service? I want a Johnny Walker Blue, and all they have is Glenfiddich in the bar fridge. I'm going to the bar.' A response came from a woman, and she sounded much younger. 'But it's the first night of our honeymoon, and you said you wanted to stay in.' The man laughed.

Rose stepped back inside, and contemplated what to do next, then remembered the earbud and wondered if Nic had the receiver turned on. Rose tapped the unit and was able to overhear a muted conversation, but there was a lot of background noise. It sounded like a troupe rehearsing for a show. Nic's voice then came through clearly. Rose could just make out the voice of another person. *'How much do you want me to take off?'* Nic replied 'All of it,' but the next response was muffled so Rose listened intensely hoping for a better reception. It sounded like: *"Everything, it has to be everything, the more the better."*

Rose wondered what Nic was getting up to, so she located the Cruising Daily Brochure on the coffee table and read about tonight's performance. It was an improvised version of the Swan Lake ballet and the performance was due to start in two hours. Rose smiled at the thought of seeing Nic dressed in a tutu.

After showering and finding a suitable outfit for her first night experience of onboard dining, Rose stepped out from her suite and noticed a pink Post-It note in the "letter box" by her door. It was Nic's handwriting. It read: "Single Ready to Mingle @ 7– see you there." Rose sighed and realised this meant she would be avoiding her first-night dining and theatrical experience, so she went back inside the cabin to change to something less formal, and nibbled from the fresh fruit and cheese platter to ease her hunger pangs.

Around an hour later, Rose arrived at the rooftop bar where the single/mingle function was happening. Nic was again shrouded by a group of women and they were all sipping from champagne flutes. Rose found a seat at the bar and her earbud begun chirping, so she casually rubbed her ear to try lessen the noise. Nic joined her and he called over to the barman. 'I believe that last drink was Bombay, Sir. Do you have something with a little more something?'

The barman leaned toward Nic. 'That wasn't gin, Sir. It was sparkling water with a touch of lime, as you instructed.' Nic raised his glass. 'Live dangerously my man, serve me the Grey Goose this time.' The barman whispered again. 'Is that code for Evian with a touch of lemon?'

Nic subtly tapped at the side of his nose and nodded. 'What happens on the cruise, stays on the cruise, my man. Fill it up.'

Rose began repeatedly tapping at her ear and finally Nic noticed so he pressed his watch to stop the noise. He then leaned toward Rose. 'Can I interest you in a champagne, young lady?'

Rose kept her gaze forward. 'No, thank you. I'm sticking to water.'

Nic grinned. 'Where's the fun in that?'

Rose shrugged and Nic held out his hand. 'Nicolai Epine, at your service.'

Rose shook his hand. 'Rosalinda.'

'No surname?'

'Nope, not yet. If I see you again, maybe we'll get to that.'

'There are only two and a half thousand people on board, plus five hundred staff. I think we'll run into each other again.'

Rose shook her head. 'I doubt it.' Nic bowed 'It will be your loss,' then he gathered his glass and returned to the horde of mingling singles.

5

Time had passed slowly for Rose sitting alone, so she began scrolling on her phone looking at the list of daily cruise events as a young woman walked in and sat down at the bar. It was Amethyst Davey. Rose moved toward her, taking the adjacent seat. 'Hello, I'm Rosalinda.'

'Amethyst, but call me Aime. First time cruising?'

'No, but first time by myself. I ...my -ex...he um...never mind.'

They continued to sit in silence when Rose noticed Aime was staring at the people behind her reflected in the full-length bar mirror. Rose realised her gaze was particularly on Nic. 'Do you know him?' Aime quickly responded. 'Who?'

'The man you keep staring at in the mirror.'

Aime pulled from her pocket a pink Post-It note. 'No, but he gave me this as I was boarding. I thought I was special.' Rose extracted her note and put it onto the bar. 'I've got one too. Snap.'

Suddenly, Aime's gaze shifted away from the mirror and Rose realised it was because Nic had seen her looking at him. He was now coming over, and he put his glass on the bar and called over the barman. 'Fill her up again, thanks.' He sat down beside Rose. 'Ah, Rosalinda, we meet again.' Rose shook her head. 'Um...sorry I've forgotten your name already.' Nic grinned. 'Nicolai Epine.'

Aime then picked up the two Post-It notes, screwed them up, and tossed them behind the bar. 'Well, Nicolai Epine. I'm Aime. I thought you'd specially invited me to join you here, and now I find you handed them out to everyone else.'

'Welcome aboard, Aime. Everyone is special on this cruise.'

Nic then leaned forward, picked up Rose's phone, softly took her hand and placed her thumb on the sensor to open it, then held it out in front of the three of them. 'Selfie'... then put it back onto the bar.

Rose snatched the phone back. 'Hands off, Mr Ep....whoever you are.'

The barman then handed Nic his drink. 'As you ordered Sir, but please be aware we do not tolerate excessive drunkenness on board, so this will be your last.' Nic sipped the drink, winked, and returned to the singles crowd.

Rose continued to watch Nic in the reflection of the bar mirror. 'I was wondering if he had something to do with the cruise. We caught an Uber from the city together, but he didn't say anything, and he stiffed me on sharing the fare.'

Aime nodded. 'Men. Can't live with them and can't live without them.'

'You don't have to tell me. I bought this care of my -ex.' Rose pulled on her necklace chain. 'I gave myself a present when my divorce settlement finally went through.'

'May I?' Aime softly caressed the white gold and diamond-encrusted chain. 'From Tiffany, in Brisbane?' Rose smiled. 'Not quite, Las Vegas. I shouted myself to a trip over there when the money came through

Aime nodded. 'Are you a gambler?'

'Just learning.'

Aime grinned. 'I can teach you. There are casino tables on board.' Rose nodded. 'I know, but I read that we have to wait until we are twelve nautical miles from port. They don't open it until we get out to sea.'

'Not quite. I noticed your cruise card was for one of The Mansion Suites, so you would have access to the VIP tables.' Rose downed the last of her drink. 'Well, I have been snacking on the hors d'oeuvres and I am looking for something a little more. Can we eat up there?' Aime stood and smiled. 'Of course. Let me show you Level 10.'

Aime led Rose from the bar and they headed for the VIP area. They stopped at a designated escalator, and Aime held out her pass. 'You need to wave your card over the door panel for access as it's restricted, and very exclusive.'

The elevator arrived and a hostess stepped out dressed in a black suit. 'Welcome back, Ms Davey,' then she held out her hand to Rose. 'Welcome, I am Gigi. I believe you are Ms Jardin.'

Rose held up her hands defensively. 'I am, but please no surnames. Please call me Rosalinda.'

Gigi nodded. 'Apologies Rosalinda.'

The hostess selected UP, they ascended, and the trip took no longer than two seconds. Gigi stepped out, holding the doors for Aime and Rose, and another hostess approached them. 'Welcome to "The Cloud". It is exclusive use for you and your guests. Please be aware that only one guest is allowed at any one time. You must always carry your pass on you and you will have complete privacy here. Anything is available at your request, but the impossible takes a little longer.'

Aime smiled. 'And our table is ready, already.'

Rose and Aime were led to a Roulette table. Rose sighed. 'Sorry Aime, I thought we were dining?'

Aime nodded. 'We are, but first I just want to drop something on black. It's the shortest odds at fifty/fifty.'

Rose leaned forward to view to table odds. 'Not exactly. You could also bet odds or even too, it's about the same, but the house generally wins. We have a better chance at winning with Blackjack.'

Aime nodded. 'I know, but I'm thinking as we're on a cruise, the house has already won with what they charged us to be onboard.' Aime then zipped open her handbag and placed five thousand dollars cash on the table. The croupier replaced the cash with five single thousand-dollar gold chips and tapped at the bet. Aimie placed two thousand on black and placed the other three chips into a large handbag.

The croupier called out, 'No more bets,' and spun the wheel. The ball dropped into Red 5, so he placed a black marble marker on the table number and called out. 'No winners.'

Rose handed over her VIP card. 'Straight up. Five hundred on Red number 5.'

The croupier nodded and placed the purple chip on the table at Number 5. Aime had noticed. "That's a thirty-five to one win on a number that's just been drawn. Unlikely, but I like your style, Rosalinda.'

Rose smiled. 'Actually, the odds are around thirteen hundred to one to get the same number twice in a row, but it will pay eighteen grand and buy me half of a matching bracelet for this necklace if I win.'

Rose rubbed the chain for good luck, the wheel was spun at it stopped at black, number 6. 'Close, but not close enough. Anyway, can we eat, please, Aime? I'm famished.'

Aime nodded and held up a finger. 'As I said before, our table is ready, already. Care to join me?' Immediately, another hostess approached them. 'Please follow me. We have had the Bollinger on ice upon your arrival.' The hostess looked at Rose. 'I am aware that you do not partake in alcoholic consumption. Can we offer you a Glaceau instead?'

Rose nodded. 'Bollinger will be fine, thank you. I decided to drink water at the bar in case of um…' Rose decided not to complete the sentence and allowed the hostess to continue. 'You had the Singapore Sling mocktail on Level 9. Please accept my apologies for the assumption.' She softly clapped her hands twice and two flutes of Bollinger were poured and handed to them.

They arrived at their table where a chef was waiting: 'For entrée, our Diver scallops will be served with blanched green beans and buttery sliced almonds, and for mains, the Wagyu is a fine choice. It is prepared finely sliced and served with a light sauce made from butter, herbs, and garlic. Maxime, our sommelier, will offer you a choice of wine to accompany the experience.'

The Chef clapped his hands and Maxime approached them. 'We have specially chosen a Henschke Hill of Grace 2019 for you tonight.'

Both of the staff then quickly excused themselves, and Aime grinned. 'I never get tired of being treated like a princess. I guess this is all new for you, Rosalinda?'

Rose nodded. 'I could get used to it, but I might have to ask my lawyer for a review of my divorce settlement.'

While they were waiting for the meal, Aime stood up. 'Please excuse me for a moment I have to use the ladies' room. They're always just outside the restaurants whenever you need them. Enjoy the champagne and, of course, the view.'

Rose watched her exit and called the sommelier over to the table. 'Can we have fresh glasses please?' The hostess nodded. 'Of course, just this time or each time we pour the champagne.'

'Actually, can you make mine sparkling water with a tiny twist of lime? Please continue to serve it in the flute, and make sure it is comparable to the colour of the Bollinger. My friend will continue with the champagne.'

The hostess appeared a little puzzled, nodded, and moved away. Aime returned a few moments later, and the meals were quietly served. Rose stayed with her "champagne" and decided the entre was sufficient to curb her hunger.

As their conversations had mainly been around the food and the cruise, Rose took the opportunity to segue into Aime's background and hopefully reveal where the investigation may be headed. 'Aime, you certainly live well. Apart from gambling, do you have other vices I need to know before I'm led astray?'

Aime smiled. 'Gold.'

Rose grinned. 'That's something else I should look into. Anyway, given it's my first night and all, I think I'll head off to my cabin. I'll see you around.'

Aime nodded. 'I'm sure you'll find me on the ship somewhere.'

6

The following morning Rose carefully opened the cabin door expecting it to be shrouded with a birthday banner as she had read it was customary for cruise ships to celebrate the birthdays of their passengers. Fortunately, there wasn't, so Rose went for a pre-breakfast amble around the ship to walk off any over-indulgence from last night's indulgences, although her "champagne" had only left a slight heartburn from the lime juice.

Rose had also spent time online investigating Aime's and Davida's background, and discovered they were implicated in the alleged theft of four hundred ingots from the Perth Mint. The gold was still missing.

On her fourth lap of the track, Rose noticed Aime standing inside the foyer by the VIP escalator, decided to ignore her, and returned to her suite. Rose was again relieved of the absence of the birthday banner, opened the door, and stepped inside.

Nic was sitting on the lounge suite holding a cupcake with a single candle. He lit the candle and then blew it out. 'Happy 30th birthday, cupcake.'

Rose shook her head. 'Damn you, Nic. It's not my birthday, the date on my cruise registration showed it was last month. Besides, how did you get in here?'

Nic shrugged. 'How was your dinner date with your new BFF, Amethyst Davey?'

Rose sighed. 'Interesting. When I left she was very drunk and trying to kiss everybody, including the sous-chef, so I returned to my suite for some research before we lost network. How much do you know about them?'

Nic was coy with his response. 'Not as much as you, by the sounds of it.'

Rose looked at him. 'I doubt that. I have two questions for you. How much time am I supposed to spend with her?' Nic shrugged again, and Rose continued. 'It's just there's so much more to do on a cruise than sitting around sipping champagne and eating.'

Nic nodded. 'What like?'

'Shuffleboard, mini-golf, corn-hole and ignoring people sitting alone drinking at the bar.'

Nic smiled. 'What's the other question?'

Rose tapped at her ear. 'You said that my earpiece would beep if you got too close. It didn't make a sound, yet here you are.'

'I turned the function off. Anyway, I'm not here, I'm invisible. I'll leave it to you to decide how to get closer to them, but just a heads up, there may be other players that we're not aware of, and I suspect they would be keeping a close eye on your new BFF.'

Rose nodded. 'Well, get out of here then. I'd like to change for breakfast.' Nic grinned. 'I hope you like the couture in your wardrobe. I specially chose it for the cruise.'

Rose sighed. 'I don't think so, Sandy told me about it.'

'Well, she chose it, but I had to collect it from the warehouse and arrange for it to be delivered to your cabin, then I watched as they hung it up in the wardrobe.'

Rose looked to the door. 'I think it's time you left, and thanks for the cupcake, cupcake.'

Nic stood, moved to the balcony door, stepped outside, and Rose followed him. 'Where are you going? It's a bit of a leap from up here and you might get wet.'

Nic opened his hand and revealed a T-shaped metal key. 'I'm going out this way. They use this key to open the walls to wash down the decks and it allows me to move along the balconies.' He placed the key into a small hole in the wall, it clicked and he pushed it away from him. 'Oh, by the way, Rosalinda, please make sure you lock your balcony door when leaving your suite, you never know who is trying to get in.'

Rose shook her head. 'I do. So, how did you really get in?'

'I came in through the bathroom window protected by a silver spoon.'

'No, you didn't, there's no window in there.'

'OK then, I was waiting at your door with the cupcake. The housekeeper assumed it was for your birthday, so act surprised if you get a little surprise a little later.'

Rose sighed. 'Get out, well through, and don't ever come back into my suite.'

Nic smiled, closed the wall behind him, and a few moments later he stepped back into the internal passageway via the exit door. Rose returned inside her suite, locked the balcony door, and moved through the cabin to open the door. Nic was heading up the aisle. 'And stay out of this area. This is reserved for VIPs, not riff-raff like you.'

Nic turned and gave a mock salute then kept walking backwards. The cabin door in the adjacent suite opened, and a woman in her mid-thirties stepped out. 'Howdy neighbour, I'm Leyla. I was wondering what all the noise was about. Do you know that guy? You sounded annoyed with him.'

Rose shrugged. 'I think his name is ... actually, I can't remember. He introduced himself at the singles soiree.'

Leyla nodded. 'Oh, I saw him waiting at your door with a cupcake, and the housekeeper let him into your suite. Is it your birthday?'

'No, he told me the cupcake was an apology for his behaviour last night at the bar. I told him he didn't need to, and I said I don't want to see him again.'

Leyla grinned. 'That's going to be hard as we're on a ship. Anyway, if he comes back, I can get my husband to have a little word with him, and he won't bother you anymore.'

'Thanks, but I'll just go down to Guest Services and let them know.'

'OK, nice to meet you...um...you didn't say your name.'

'It's Rosalinda.'

Leyla smiled. 'Well, Rosalinda, it's nice to meet you. My husband's name is Rocky, you can't miss him. He's about six foot six and built like a WWE wrestler.'

Rose nodded. 'What does he do?'

'He's a retired WWE wrestler. He used to be known as Rocky Mountain.'

Leyla stepped back into her cabin and returned a few moments later with a business card. 'Here, please take this. It's got my phone number on it, so if you want to join us at dinner or anything, just send me a text.'

Rose turned to re-enter her suite. 'Thanks, I'll keep that in mind. I'll see you around.' Leyla grinned. 'Please, let me know if we get too loud. We're on our honeymoon, and these walls aren't that thick.'

Rose turned back. 'I heard you this morning.'

Leyla raised her hand to her mouth. 'I'm so sorry.'

'No, nothing like that. I overheard your husband complaining about the lack of liquor choice in the bar fridge and about the casino not yet being open. That's not exactly true, as we are in VIP suites there's a casino on Level 10 just for us.'

Leyla grinned. 'I wondered where he went. I was in the bathroom getting ready, and he was watching the television. He stood up suddenly, and I thought he said something about getting something for his back. Now that I think of it, he said he was putting something on black.'

Rose nodded. 'There's roulette tables, poker tables, and a couple of pokies too. I was up there last night with another passenger. She told me about it. I might see you there sometime.' Leyla nodded. 'Thanks for that.'

Rose smiled, put the card in her pocket, and stepped back into her cabin.

Around twenty minutes later, Rose was at breakfast admiring the view when she noticed Nic approaching her. He didn't make eye contact but feigned a bump on her table and moved further along without an apology, however, he had left an empty glass.

Rose noticed it had a Post-it note attached to the bottom and called the nearest waiter over. 'Would you mind clearing my table, please?' The attendant nodded and collected the dishes, but Rose managed to retain the note. It read: "Aft Level 2 Take lift 3. Be there in 4."

As the breakfast restaurant was at the stern, she moved quickly from the area and headed for the set of lifts outside the eatery, took the first one available and selected down thinking it would be easier to traverse the ship as they should be less people at the lower levels. Rose arrived and saw Nic was in one of them. It stopped on Level 2, the doors opened, and Nic smiled at her. There was no one else in the lift. Rose stepped in, still catching her breath, and tapped at her ear as it had begun to buzz. 'What's the emergency? We're supposed to be ignoring each other, and you know I hate to run.'

Nic pressed Level 10, kept looking straight ahead, and began to speak softly. 'My Spidey senses tell me that I'm being tailed, and I don't like people playing pin the tail on Nicky. I think I'll have to make myself invisible.' Nic pressed his watch to deactivate Rose's earpiece.

Rose smiled. 'Finally, you're revealing your alter-ego, you're a donkey.' Nic shrugged, squatted down, and re-tied his shoelaces. 'It could be the guy in the suite next to you. I took a picture of him with my phone, and Chewy is doing a facial thing on him.'

Nic then stood up, leaned forward, and inserted a key into the lift board. It came to a momentary stop. 'Be careful.'

Rose whispered. 'I met her. She said her name was Leyla, and her husband's name was Rocky Mountain. He's an ex-wrestler. I don't think he's interested in you.'

'Have you met him?'

Rose whispered again. 'No, but why would they be tailing you?'

Nic restarted the lift. 'Chewy did some more digging on the missing gold. This is the big league, and with that sort of coin, you can easily get some very nasty people to look out for you.' Rose nodded again. 'So what do you want me to do?'

'Just keep playing it as planned. We're not due to arrive in Sydney until tomorrow night. I'll make a decision then.'

The lift arrived at Level 10, the doors opened and a hostess stepped forward to acknowledge their arrival. 'Welcome back, Rosalinda. I see you have another guest with you. He will also be welcome.'

Rose glared at Nic. 'I don't know this man. He keeps following me.' Rose then entered the VIP lounge and approached the nearest poker table. The hostess had held the doors to help her through, then held them a little longer, and addressed Nic: 'Sir, this is an exclusive area of the ship. You are not permitted to enter without authorisation.' Nic shrugged, pressed Level 5, and the doors closed.

Rose noticed Aime was sitting at one of the tables, so she wandered over expecting that she had seen her arrive. Aime smiled. 'Is he still hanging around? I thought you gave him the flick after the singles thing.'

'I did, but we're on a ship. I guess it's hard to avoid people.'

Aime nodded. 'I've got access to some people on board that can take care of pesky passengers like him.' Rose shook her head. 'I think he's harmless, maybe a little lonely, but harmless. Besides, we've only been on board a day so I'm sure he'll find a lonely heart, or a nurse with a purse somewhere after he gives up on pursuing me.

Aime nodded. 'I guess so, and there are lots of single ladies or desperate men looking for company. You can find them sitting alone at meal times.'

Rose smiled. 'I'll make sure I find someone to eat with me then.'

Aime nodded again. 'You could always dine with me. I'm putting a table together of like-minded people so we can all get to know each other. I'll be happy to reserve a chair for you.'

'Thanks, I'll think about it. How do I get in touch apart from coming in here?'

'I'm in Mansion Suite 4, and you're in 9, so I'm sure we'll see each other in the aisle. If not, just ring my suite and leave a message. I'm about to head off to join in with the Trivia Quiz Competition. It starts in about ten minutes. Are you any good at trivia?'

Rose was a little guarded with her response, not wanting to overplay anything. 'I can hold my own as long as there aren't any questions on music, movies, history, geography or general knowledge.'

Aime grinned. 'It doesn't matter anyway; the alcohol is on tap, and we don't have to drive home. Besides that, I've heard that the prizes are pretty lame.'

They were heading toward the upper deck entertainment area where the game would be played and Rose happened to notice a large man in her peripheral vision. 'Sorry, Aime, can we stop for a second? I've just seen an emerald in the jeweller shop; I'd love to know how much it is.'

Aime stopped and Rose noticed the man had stopped as well. He quickly took out his phone, started tapping on it, and turned away. Rose then gained the jeweller's attention. 'I'm interested in the emerald. Is it for sale or just an exhibition piece?'

The salesperson was very eager to show her. 'This is called Serenitea. It's Columbian, AAA quality, and one of the finest stones we've ever had in our catalogue. We can arrange it to fit any piece of your design.'

Rose nodded. 'I have been looking for an emerald for quite some time, ever since I saw the earrings worn by Angelina at the 2009 Oscars. I believe they were designed by Lorraine Schwartz and around a hundred carats.'

The salesperson smiled. 'You know your emeralds, Ms Jardin.'

Rose nodded. 'That I do. Green is my favourite colour too.'

Aime smiled. 'And I will be green with envy if you buy it.'

The jeweller carefully removed the stone from the glass case and laid it onto a black velvet swathe. 'Note the vivid colour saturation. This one is around twenty-seven carats, which would cost around forty thousand American dollars.'

Aime leaned forward. 'That's about sixty grand in Aussie.' Rose nodded and stepped back from the jeweller. 'I'll leave it for the moment, thank you. If it is still here when we arrive in Perth, I'll make a decision then.' The salesperson was obviously disappointed. 'It's not going to Perth. We are dropping off in Sydney for an exhibition. I'll need a decision soon, Ms Jardin.'

Rose smiled and stepped backward into the aisle. 'That's fine, a stone like that will not be hard to track down in Sydney once it leaves the ship.'

Aime had now joined her, but Rose held out her hand to stop her from moving any further. 'There's a man following us.'

'What, who?'

'The big guy standing behind us. He's been talking into his phone, but there's no network as we're too far out to sea.'

Aime nodded. 'Do you want me to talk to him?'

'Do you know him?'

'Yes. He's my bodyguard.' Rose hesitated. 'Rocky Mountain?'

Aime looked at her. 'What's that?'

'His name.'

'No, it's..... we brought him with us as we're carrying so much cash.'

They started to walk along the tiled corridor, and Rose realised Aime had said "we" and "us." 'Who is we and us?' Aime looked around. 'Um...sorry I meant me.' Rose nodded again. 'Why did you bring cash with you as everything can go onto the Cruise Card?' Aime slowed her gait. 'The VIP Casino accepts cash as well as the card. Cash is easier to deal with, as once you use it all, you stop.

Also, you can exchange the cash for the chips and they don't ask any questions.'

'Where do you keep all the cash?'

Aime had stopped walking. 'You ask a lot of questions, Rosalina. Are you planning to rob me?'

Rose sighed. 'No, it's just it seems a little...'

'Dangerous?'

'No, I wasn't going to say that. Surely, it would be traceable. Doesn't the onboard casino still have to complete those Anti-Money Laundering reports?'

Aime looked at Rose. 'You ask too many questions, Rosalinda. I've changed my mind. My table at the Quiz is already full and I don't think there's room for one more.' Aime quickly moved away, with her bodyguard following closely behind.

Rose considered returning to her suite but decided to attend the quiz regardless of what had just transpired with Aime. Rose arrived at the entertainment deck, ignored Aime's group, gathered a pencil and scoresheet from the emcee, found a spare seat, and sat down.

The emcee began the presentation: 'Ladies and Gentlemen, thank you for coming along to our first quiz. Today's topic is Musicals, but before we get started has every group collected a scoresheet and pencil?' There was a chorus of 'Yes', and a few latecomers wandered over to her to get a scoresheet.

'We start in two minutes. Just a few rules before we get underway. The groups are limited to six players, and should there be any singles out there, please look around to see if you would like to join up with some others. I will say the question once only, then repeat it as required at the end of the quiz.' There were a couple of table rearrangements, but no one came toward to join Rose.

The emcee clapped her hands. 'OK, let's get down to it. The first question is about' but before she could complete it someone from the crowd stood up and pointed towards Aime's table. 'They have eight people.' There was a murmur of agreement amongst the crowd and Aime stood up. 'We're two groups of four, so sit back down and stop your whinging.'

Rose wondered what was going to happen next and noticed Aime's bodyguard had moved in front of the interjector. He put both hands on his table, and the man sat down quickly.

The emcee continued: *'Question 1. It's an easy one....What is the name of the hit song from the 2013 movie, Frozen?'*

Rose wrote down the answer, sat back, and noticed a man of undeterminable age was approaching her table. He was using a cane and dragging his left leg. 'Are you on your own young lady? Do you mind if I join you?'

Rose's earpiece had begun to lightly buzz as the man sat down. They shook hands and the man gave a toothless grin. He didn't offer his name. 'Did you answer the first question correctly?' Rose nodded.

'Question 2. When the musical Mame opened on Broadway in 1966, which actress played the lead role?' Rose wrote down Angela Lansbury.

A loud hub-hub came from Aime's table as the group argued about the name. The man who had interjected previously called out to them. 'Surely, between the eight of you, you know the answer is Lucille Ball.' There was a groan from the others in the room, and the man grinned. 'Or was it?'

'Question 3. 'How many times has the Film 'A Star is Born' been made?'

Rose took a moment, and her quiz partner began counting them on his fingers. 'My dear old mamma saw the first one in 1937. I would say four.' Rose wrote 4.

'Question 4. The first musical on Broadway was The Black Crook. In what year?'

The man leaned forward. 'You know, I think my great-grandpappy was in that.'

Rose shook her head and leaned forward. 'I don't think so. Excellent disguise by the way Nic, but I was hoping you'd remain invisible. Although you do look a bit like an older version of the guy from the Pretty Woman movie, and the round silver-rimmed glasses are a good touch. Do they blur your vision?'

The man stood up. 'All the gear and no idea who this Nic is. I'm sorry, little lady, I have to visit the little boy's room.' He gathered his cane and began to shuffle away. Rose called out to him. 'Remember your limp is on the left side, and can you please turn off the buzzing noise in my ear, Mr No Idea.'

The man hadn't returned by the time they were up to the ninth question and Rose wondered if he'd managed to get himself stuck in the toilet. She decided to leave and found him standing by the lift lobby.

'You saw through my disguise?'

Rose shook her head. 'Really? That's the first question that comes to mind. What about that we've been working together for the last three years, solving nearly twenty scams, attempted frauds, and other stuff, and you think I can't work out it's you under all that silicon mask?'

Nic shrugged. 'The Harry Potter's Cloak of Invisibility was already taken.'

Rose nodded. 'Besides that, my earpiece started buzzing, and it's very annoying. Can you please turned it off as we keep running into each other.' Nic tapped at this watch, the buzzing stopped and Rose rubbed her ear. 'Thanks, so what do you want me to do now?'

Nic whispered. 'You have to remain chummy with your new BFF before she kicks you to the kerb and finds someone else to gloat to about the gold'

Rose nodded. 'What about the bodyguard? Was he the guy following you?'

'Yep. I must have really annoyed her with the Post-It note thing. He's already had a go at Nicolai.' Rose quizzed him. 'You mean you?'

Nic shrugged. 'No, I mean Nicolai Epine, I don't think he's met the new me.'

They took the next lift and went through the ship to the eatery and sat down at a table for two in the outside area by the swimming pool. It was warm enough for Rose not to need a jacket. The sea swell was light, and the nearby swimming pool was empty of any swimmers. Nic leaned forward. 'Would you like the good news or the bad news?' Rose shrugged. 'Either, it doesn't matter.' Nic continued. 'Well, the bad news is I've decided to stay onboard the ship.'

Rose shook her head. 'So what's the good news?'

Nic grinned. 'You've found someone to dine with, so you won't get lonely.'

They'd been sitting there for about half an hour when a waiting staff approached them and offered to re-fill their coffee cups, then began to explain the lunch menu. Rose nodded. 'Thank you. Oh, and can you please bring my friend here a drinking straw, he can only have smoothies for lunch as he has no teeth.' The staff member looked a little puzzled. 'I don't think we have any straws, but I can mush up some peas and carrots to make it easier for him, or I can get the chef to prepare gazpacho.'

Rose smiled. 'Either would be good, thank you.'

The staff member moved away, and Nic pulled a small box from his pocket then placed it on the table. 'I have a present for you.' Rose looked at it. 'You said we weren't doing my birthday and you didn't bother to wrap it.'

Nic nodded. 'Open it.' Rose lifted the small box and rattled it. 'Can I eat it?'

'Nup. Well, you could, but it might give you a major stomach ache.'

'Can I wear it? Is it a tiny hat?'

Nic smiled. 'You'll have to wait and see.'

Rose opened the box, and inside was a green emerald, identical to the one she'd been looking at with Aime. 'You bought the emerald?'

'Not exactly.'

Nic suddenly leaned forward, gathered the emerald, and quickly placed it back into the box as Aime was approaching their table. Rose looked up at her. 'Did you win? It all got too hard for me.' They didn't offer her a chair, and Aime ignored the question. 'I see you've found a friend.'

Rose nodded and realised Nic hadn't offered his name. 'This is...'

Nic stood up. 'Nice to meet you, Davit Poole is the name. I'm Rosalinda's ex-husband's lawyer. I didn't know she was on the cruise until I saw her upstairs doing the quiz. She looked a little lonely so I joined her, but my bladder gave in so I had to leave. I hope I haven't stolen her away from you.' Nic sat down but as he did he accidentally tipped the coffee cup onto the floor and the hot liquid splashed onto Aime's shoes. 'Oops, sorry, I'm so clumsy. My tired old hands aren't what they used to be.' Aime shook the spillage from her shoe and remained standing.

Nic re-started the conversation with Rose, extended his hand to place it on top of Rose's and they continued to ignore Aime. 'Dearest Rosalinda, it only seems like yesterday we were dealing with that ugly divorce court thing.'

Rose quickly pulled her hand back. 'Have you seen him since?'

Nic smiled as best he could through silicon lips. 'Yes, it was at the Casino in Brisbane. He was there to explain to them how he would pay them back after the divorce settlement went through.'

Aime finally gave up. 'Well, I'll leave you two alone to get more acquainted. By the way Davit, you do remind me of someone.'

Nic ran his hand through his full grey wig. 'People tell me I look a little like the guy from the Pretty Woman movie, but I can't see the resemblance. We do share the same birthday, but he was born in '49, and I was born in 58.'

Aime began to leave, then turned around to look at Rose. 'That's not it, but no doubt I'll see you both around on the ship. What did you decide to do about the emerald?'

Nic smiled. 'We were just talking about it, and she's going to buy it. Rosalinda has made an appointment to meet with them at two o'clock today. Would you like to join us?'

Aime nodded. 'Sure, if I've got nothing else to do.'

Aime finally moved away, and Rose leaned forward. 'Davit Poole? What sort of name is that?'

Nic shrugged. 'I panicked. By the way, did you know the hoists holding up the lifeboats are called davits?'

Rose nodded. 'I do.'

Nic smiled. 'Can you guess how I came up with the name pool?'

Rose shook her head. 'It might have something to do with that big blue box full of water directly behind you. Why did you ask her to join us?'

'You'll see.'

Rose shrugged. 'Can I ask another question?'

'Sure, as long as it's not about choosing a better name.'

Rose sighed. 'How are you going to move around the ship without someone asking you who you are?

Davit Poole didn't board the boat.' Nic nodded. 'You only need to show ID when boarding the boat, not while you're on it.'

Rose was about to ask another question but thought better of it. 'I'll see you at the jeweller in about two hours then. I'm going to take a walk.'

7

Two hours later Rose was at the jewellery shop and shown to a "Reserved" seat at the front of the counter. Nic, still disguised as Davit, stood beside her and Aime mooched her way through the crowd to stand next to him. There were at least ten other people were milling around drinking champagne waiting for the show to begin.

The jeweller called everyone to attention: 'Ladies and Gentlemen, thank you all for coming. This is a very exciting opportunity here today as we have someone interested in buying our emerald, Serenitea. It's currently the most desirable one on the market.'

There were a few 'oohs and ahs' and the gathered crowd moved a little closer, then the jeweller continued: 'This lovely passenger here, Rosalinda, has offered the asking price, and we are pleased to say the current owners have accepted.'

Rose nodded and handed over a Credit Card instead of the onboard card. 'This will cover it. Hopefully, I get a good exchange rate.' The crowd started clapping in appreciation.

Nic leaned forward, took hold of the stone, removed a green leather bound loupe from his pocket, thumbed open the viewing glass, and peered through it at the emerald. 'Very noice. I believe it is what you have been looking for Rosalinda,' but as he handed it to Rose, the emerald slipped from his hand, bounced on the table and dropped onto the floor.

The gathered crowd let out an anxious cry, but as it bounced, Nic caught it and then passed it back to the jeweller. 'Oops, terribly sorry, my tired old hands aren't as good as they used to be.' Nic then put the loupe back into his pocket and managed to elbow Aime in the process. 'Oops, terribly sorry madam, my arms don't work as well as they used to either.'

The jeweller took a deep breath and rubbed the stone carefully with a tissue. 'No harm done, no harm done. It fell onto the carpet. We'll be keeping it in safe storage until we dock in Perth. Thank you all for coming.'

The crowd clapped again.

Nic and Rose began to move away, and Aime leaned into Rose. 'I saw that.'

Rose looked around. 'Saw what? We've got to go. I'll see you later, Aime.' Rose collected the credit card and receipt, took Nic by the arm, and headed off, but Aime kept following them. 'How do you think you'll get away with it?'

Nic stopped and turned to look at her. 'I don't know what you think you saw young lady, but all I did was drop the stone.' Aime grinned. 'You swapped it and put it in your pocket. I saw a flash of green. The jeweller didn't notice when you handed it back, but I did.'

Nic ignored the comment, moved over to the other side of the aisle, and Aime continued. 'You won't get away with it. I'll let them know. Unless....' Nic leaned toward her. 'Unless what? You're going to get your flunky to frisk an old man just in case he's carrying a sixty thousand dollar emerald in his underwear?' Nic then put his hand into his pocket and removed the green loupe. 'You mean this?'

Aime looked at the loupe and then back at Nic. 'It's in the other pocket. I'm not stupid.' Nic pulled the insides of his pockets from the trousers and they were both empty. Rose then took Nic's arm again. 'Please leave us alone.'

Aime continued to badger them. 'I'll get them to test the emerald for authenticity, and they'll know they have a fake.' Nic sighed. 'Whatever, get them to test it, but why would you do that?'

Aime stood her ground. 'Because I don't like you and I don't trust her.'

Rose began to move further along the aisle and noticed Aime's bodyguard coming towards them.

Aime beckoned for the man to come forward, and Rose sighed this time. 'Here comes the cavalry.'

The behemoth of a man had taken most of the room in the narrow passageway and now stood beside Aime. He didn't speak, and Aime continued: 'I was standing next to you and saw the switch.'

Nic looked the man up and down, then smiled. 'You know, the bigger they are, the harder they...' Nic didn't need to complete the sentence as Aime added: 'Hit.' Nic nodded. 'I was going to say fall, but I think he would hit pretty hard too.' Rose looked at Aime. 'You can't keep us from returning to my suite Aime, even with Hulk standing beside you.'

Nic grinned and tried to palm the man out of the way, but the giant didn't budge or grunt or do anything. The man slowly removed Nic's hand from his chest and Nic continued: 'Aime, can you please tell Mr Hulk here to let us through.' Aime nodded and let them continue along the aisle.

A couple of minutes later Rose and Nic arrived at her suite. Nic went into the spare room and returned a few moments later with an emerald in his hand. 'That was getting a bit uncomfortable.'

Rose nodded. 'I was expecting him to frisk you. Where did you hide it?' Nic grinned. 'There's a hole in my pocket, and it slipped straight through into my underwear. I had it all under control.'

Rose grimaced. 'Eeww. I didn't need to know that.' Nic continued: 'I was talking about the emerald, not the thing with Hulk and Aime.'

Rose nodded. 'I knew that, and I also know that you still have the fake emerald.'

'You know me too well, Rosalinda, after all, I am your only friend on the cruise.'

'No, you're not.'

'Well, apart from Aime, I am your only friend on this cruise and now that we're alone, I'll run through the rest of the plan.'

Rose sighed. 'I'm glad you have a plan with this one, most of the time I don't find out what's happening until I am part of the plan.' Rose sat down, leaned forward, and took an apple from the fruit basket, bit into it, then offered it to Nic. 'Would you like some?'

Nic shook his head. 'No thanks, I don't have any teeth.' He then moved toward the fruit basket and rustled through it until he found an avocado. 'Good, I hoped they'd put one in.' He took out the paring knife and sliced the fruit in half, removed the core, dropped the emerald in the crater, and carefully placed the two halves together. 'That will keep it safe for a while'

Rose shook her head. 'What if I want to have guacamole?'

'You might have to order in.'

'What is going to stop the avocado from getting over-ripe and mushy?'

'Boy, you ask a lot of questions.'

Rose shrugged. 'It's my job. Anyway, tell me about the rest of the plan.'

Nic was about to respond when they heard a phone ringing. 'We must be getting closer to Sydney. I wasn't expecting to be in range.'

Rose sighed. 'Did you intentionally leave your phone in here?'

Nic nodded. 'I was wondering what happened to it. I hate being old, you forget where you leave things. Now, where are my teeth?'

Rose shrugged. 'So, you did leave the phone here deliberately.'

Nic grinned, re-entered the second bedroom to answer the phone, and shut the door behind him. Rose moved out onto the balcony and a few moments later Nic re-joined her. 'That was Chewy. He let me know that he'd updated an online newsfeed about me to include - "suspected to be part of high-end gold nugget fraud in Perth."' Rose grimaced. 'Am I guilty by association?

'Yep, they are looking for a woman in her late twenties who could be thirty, who looks like you, and an elderly gentleman who looks like me, with a silicon mask that makes him look a little like the guy from the film "Pretty Woman".

Rose nodded. 'That's a very general description, so I guess we're safe for a while.'

Nic nodded. 'Would you like to see what Chewy posted?'

Rose shrugged. 'I guess.'

Nic tapped his phone and laid it down face up on the table. There was a photograph of two men standing beside a small helicopter. The eldest looking man was holding a large gold nugget in his hands. It was about the size of a fat banana. Both were smiling, and the new "Welcome to Perth Airport" sign loomed in the background.

Rose leaned a little closer. 'That looks like someone else is wearing your Davit Poole mask. When was this taken? I didn't know you'd recently been in Western Australia.'

Nic shrugged. 'Have mask will travel.'

Rose placed her forefinger and thumb onto the screen to expand the picture. 'They're not your skinny legs and he's too short to be you.' Rose slid the picture to focus on the second man. 'And if I'm not mistaken the other guy is your mate, Elvis. He flew us around in his little helicopter when we investigated that wine scam thing in Margaret River last year.'

Nic smiled. 'Well spotted. We just have to wait until your new BFF, Aime, sees the post. Chewy is sending her an anonymous Facebook link now. We'll be following it up with another post of where the nugget was discovered. Then, a little later, the two guys might be arrested on suspicion of attempted fraud involving the suspect nugget.'

Rose shook her head. 'Them? Don't you mean you? I can't wait. The nugget looks like a couple of kilos so that puts the value at around two hundred thousand. Is the nugget real?'

Nic shrugged again. 'As real as it can be at such short notice.'

Rose shook her head. 'So now I'm mixed up in a fake gold nugget and a fake emerald stone, lucky me. Are we going to get arrested when we arrive in Perth?'

Nic closed the phone. 'Not unless Aime dobs us in, but that's not going to happen.' Rose sighed. 'Why?'

'We're going to offer her the emerald.'

'The real one, or the fake one?'

Nic smiled. 'She won't know the difference unless she gets it examined by a professional. This is a good fake.'

Rose considered the comment. 'What if she takes it to the jeweller on board, won't they test it?'

Nic shook his head. 'It might be a little inappropriate to ask them to check whether the stone that she has, which looks identical to the one they have, might be a fake.'

Rose nodded. 'So, that's the plan? Sell her the fake and she gets caught red-handed in Perth when she tries to pawn it?'

'Almost, but she won't get caught. Also, Chewy is meeting us over there.'

Rose sighed. 'So, you're letting him back into the field? Last time it didn't work out so well as he kept trying to hit people with his plastic Star Wars lightsaber.'

Nic nodded. 'I know what a waste, but at least we could claim the damage on our insurance.'

Rose shook her head. 'How are we going to set up the sale of the emerald to Aime?'

Nic nodded again. 'I've been thinking about that. I think it's about time you go back to the gambling table and lose heavily. Then try to borrow some of that cash from Aime and ante up the emerald as collateral.'

Rose sighed. 'That sounds like a plan. Can I ask you another question?'

'Sure.'

'When are you taking the mask off or are you sleeping in it?

Nic shook his head and pulled at the silicon. 'I can't take it off.'

'You mean you can't, or you won't?'

'That was two questions. I can't, because it's difficult to get on and off without help, and I won't, because it makes me look old and I can get away with being grumpy all the time, and I like eating through a straw.'

'I've never thought of you as being grumpy. Happy, sleepy, and dopey, but never grumpy.'

Nic grinned. 'OK Snow White, I'll take it off later, but can you help me put it back in the morning?'

Rose nodded. 'Sure, but how will you manage to get through the ship from your cabin without a face?' Nic shrugged. 'Oh, didn't I tell you that? That's another part of the plan as I'm now staying here with you in this suite.'

The doorbell rang, Rose opened it, and a steward stood there with Nic's luggage. 'Where can I put this suitcase?'

Rose looked at him. 'Bring it in and I'll open the balcony door for you. I hope it floats.'

The steward ignored her comment, dropped the suitcases into the second bedroom, about-faced and left the cabin.

They spent the evening reviewing Plan A and Nic went into the second bedroom to try out the beds - there were two at knee level and another two folded down from the walls. He called out to Rose. 'I think I'll sleep on the floor.'

Rose responded. 'And keep your door locked.'

Nic stepped out of the room. 'And why would that be?'

Rose sighed. 'Certain people tend to enter my suite without being invited. Oh, and by the way, haven't you forgotten something?'

Nic tapped at his pockets. 'Nup, unless you want a midnight tipple.'

Rose shook her head. 'Nope, you dope, you still have the mask on.'

'Well, there is that. Can you help me take it off?'

'Sure.'

Rose stepped toward him and together they wrestled the silicon mask from his head, and it gave a resounding "pop" when it finally came off. Nic noticed Rose was staring at him. 'Stop staring. You've seen my face before.'

Rose nodded. But you're bald, and you've shaved all you hair off including your eyebrows. It's very weird in a very weird sort of way.'

Nic nodded. 'Do you know how hard it is to put on a new face every day?'

Rose shook her head. 'Well, I manage, a little bit of mascara and a splash of lippy, but I don't keep my face in a jar by the door like you do.'

8

After a late breakfast, they headed off to the private club at Level 10. Rose stepped out of the elevator and was greeted by the hostess. 'This is my...friend, Davit Poole. He likes a little flutter. I didn't know he was on board. Is he allowed to join me here?' The hostess nodded. 'Certainly. Would you like a private table?'

Rose nodded. 'That would be nice, thank you.'

The hostess smiled. 'Please follow me.'

Rose took Nic's arm, and they followed the hostess to a table allocated for Blackjack. Nic whispered to Rose. 'Say something about me having been banned from most casinos as I've been registered as a card counter.'

'Excuse me, Gigi. My friend has.... he told me he has a little issue with having been banned from some casinos. Something to do with card counting. Is that something that your casino frowns upon?' Gigi stopped and turned to face them. 'There's nothing in here that's frowned upon. If we start to lose too much, we shut the table down, but that's never happened.'

Rose nodded. 'What happens if we lose too much?'

Gigi smiled. 'That's never happened either.'

Rose and Nic took their seats, and a croupier came forward to commence the game. Rose smiled at him. 'Hello Sebastian. Please be gentle with me as it's my first time playing this game.'

The croupier nodded. 'And you, Sir?'

Nic nodded. 'Me? ... Well, I'll be watching if that's OK. I might join in later.'

The croupier opened four fresh decks of cards and placed them into an automatic shuffler. 'As there are only two of you, I'll be using only the four decks. It will raise the odds of your winning. Will that be OK?'

Nic nodded. 'Fine by me, but before you shuffle, can you please fan the cards face up as I'd like to confirm all the cards are there.'

The attendant looked at him. 'That is not needed, Sir.'

'I insist.'

Rose tapped Nic on the forearm. 'Let him do his job.' Nic sighed. 'OK, just remember the last time we went gambling Rosalinda, you dropped over ten grand in half an hour.'

The croupier ignored the comment and began to fill the dealing shoe with the cards. 'It is our policy that our passengers do not overcommit to liabilities they cannot fulfil, and we carefully investigate our special clients that have access to this private area.'

Nic smiled. 'Whales.'

Rose grinned and looked out the window. 'Where? You must have good eyesight.'

Sebastian nodded. 'We don't allow whales on board, Sir. It is not what our onboard gambling experience is all about. It is low-level betting and hopefully high returns for the passenger. Twenty dollars minimum. No Maximum.'

Rose put down a five-hundred-dollar chip, and her cards were dealt face up. They were both the Aces of Spades. The dealer placed his first card face down and then dealt himself another. It was the two of diamonds.

Nic grinned. 'Insurance?'

Sebastian looked at Nic. 'Please refrain from unnecessary comments at the table.'

Rose tapped the cards. 'I'll split them, please. I like my chances.'

'It's your first deal madam.'

'Yes, and I'm about to win twice.'

Rose tapped at her cards again and was dealt two tens. 'Double Blackjack. Looks like I'm in the money.' Nic smiled. 'Not yet. If he draws twenty-one with the next four cards, he wins.'

Sebastian nodded, turned over his card and as it was the six of clubs, he proceeded to deal another card. It was another two, then a three, another three, then five. He called out: 'Twenty-one.'

Nic shook his head. 'Five Card Charlie. Dealer wins.' Rose looked at him. 'Surely not? I've got two Blackjacks that should count for something.'

Sebastian smiled, then handed Rose three five-hundred-dollar chips. 'Player wins. It's a House Rule.'

They played for another hour, and Rose had accumulated around four thousand dollars in chips despite her attempts to deliberately over-bet at times. Nic leaned back into his chair. 'This is going to be harder than I thought.'

Rose smiled. 'Well, you know what they say...'

Nic nodded. 'Winners are grinners?'

'Nope. Lucky at cards, unlucky in love.'

Meanwhile, other players had joined in, the table was full, and everyone appeared to be winning. Rose stood up and offered her seat to another punter.

Sebastian welcomed the new player, and a new game started. He filled the shoe with another two decks and immediately dealt Blackjack to himself. 'No winners.'

Nic began to move away and then looked back at the table. 'I think you were everybody's good luck charm, but you know what this means?'

Rose shook her head 'Nope.'

'We'll have to go to plan B. Let's go back to my cabin and talk about it.'

Rose sighed. 'Don't you mean my suite?'

'Oh, no, my suite. Didn't I tell you that? Sorry, I'm getting old you know.'

They arrived at the lift, stepped in and Nic selected Floor 5. 'I'm now at Level 5. I had to change cabins as the person in the suite claimed I gnash my teeth when I sleep. I thought that was odd, as I don't have any.'

Rose nodded. 'What a shame you're no longer in my suite.'

'Nup, there's no shame in it. I stayed there while my new cabin was being cleaned. I'm now in a tiny little, weeny, tiny cabin on Level 5, all by myself.'

'You said tiny twice. I've seen the ship plan, and don't think any cabins on this level classify as tiny or weeny.'

They arrived at Nic's new cabin, and a steward was waiting for him. 'Everything is as you requested, Mr Poole.' Nic nodded. 'Thank you, Antoine.'

The steward held open the door, they stepped inside, and Rose noticed the panoramic view. The steward moved over to the bank of sliding doors and drew them open. 'They fold into each other to give you an uninterrupted view. It's one of the features of our Honeymoon Suite.'

Rose looked at Nic, who was trying to operate a spaceship-looking coffee machine. 'Nice suite, Nic…oops Davit.'

Nic then moved into his bedroom suite to change into something more comfortable and there was a knock at the door. A young woman dressed in formal black and white attire entered and moved toward the machine. 'Good morning, Madam, my name is Ophelia, and I will be your butler for the remainder of the journey. Please let me know what you need, anytime.'

Rose nodded. 'Thank you, Ophelia, however, this is my friend's suite, I'm staying in a Mansion Suite on Level 9.'

Nic called out from the other room. 'Thank you for the offer. Rosalinda will be taking care of me. She used to buttle for the Queen.' Rose curtseyed and Ophelia continued. 'Well, if you are sure, and you do not need me for anything, Antoine can keep me updated as required. Please accept my apologies for the confusion, it's not often we have a groom staying in the Honeymoon suite on their own.'

Rose shrugged. 'His new bride suffers from chronic seasickness and wasn't able to join us.' Ophelia nodded. 'Is it their first time apart since being married?'

'Yes…. I guess he should have asked her that question before he asked her the big question.'

Ophelia bowed and Nic called out again. 'Oh, sorry Ophelia, there is something you can do for me. Please locate a fellow passenger, Amethyst Davey, and have her come to my suite at two o'clock this afternoon. I have a gift for her.'

Ophelia bowed again and left the room.

It was now two o'clock and the doorbell rang. Rose stood up, made her way over to the door and peered through the peephole. 'It's Aime and it looks like she's alone. Shall I let her in?'

'Yep, but we'll keep the emerald thing on the down low at the moment.'

Rose opened the door and beckoned Aime to enter. Nic stood up and waddled his way over to her. 'Thank you for coming Aime. I think we may have got off on the wrong foot yesterday. Please take a seat. We have a proposal for you.'

Aime looked at them suspiciously. 'I think I'll stay standing, thank you, and you never mentioned you were on your honeymoon. Where is your bride?'

Nic sighed. 'Still in Brisbane.'

Aime considered the comment and added. 'So, when did you get married?'

'Last week. I didn't tell her about the honeymoon being on a cruise ship until we were leaving the Weston Hotel.'

'And?'

'She suffers from chronic seasickness, so I took a cab to the cruise ship, and she stayed in the Westin. It was our first argument.'

Aime smiled. 'And it won't be your last. Anyway, what am I here for?'

Rose sighed. 'Um, I have a little problem with a gambling debt and thought you might be able to help me out.' Aime looked at them both. 'What makes you think I can help?' Nic ignored the question. 'It appears that Rosalinda's ex-husband over-extended her credit line with his bookie in Sydney, and they've demanded payment in full within seven days.'

'So?'

Rose stepped over to join Nic. 'You mentioned you have access to some cash so we were wondering if I...um...could borrow some money.' Aime nodded. 'Hang on, you said *he* over-extended your credit line. I thought you said you were a new gambler; how did you manage to get a credit line with a bookie?'

Nic rubbed his chin. 'That's the point, Aime. He used Rosalinda's name to set it up and they didn't verify any details. They are asking her to settle the excess in full while they undertake an internal investigation.'

'So, explain to me why this is my problem?'

Nic continued. 'Well, if you could get access to about thirty thousand in cash, we could make it all go away until he gets his um...stuff worked out.'

Aime turned around and began to walk toward the door. 'As I said, why is it my problem?' Nic moved over to Rose and whispered: 'Let's show her the emerald.'

Rose took a deep breath. 'Well, I believe you mentioned you saw something at the jeweller, and we don't want any wrinkles in our um...plans.'

Aime stopped, turned, and smiled. 'So, that's your sudden interest in me.'

Nic put his hand into his pocket, removed a matchbox, and carefully placed it on the table. 'Before you take the next step, how can we be assured you can meet our requirements?' Nic didn't open the box and Aime laughed. 'You really have no idea about me, do you?'

Nic nodded, opened up his phone, and waved it towards her. 'Probably not, but please bear with me and I'll read a little of what we have found out: Your full name is Amethyst Gillian Davey, you are thirty-nine years old; you have been in a relationship with Duvad Sheloff for nine years; you do not have any children of your own however Duvad has a boy and twin girls – who are currently attending at The John Carmel College in Perth. Your Father died nine years ago while gold prospecting in Kalgoorlie. His body has not been recovered. You are travelling with your mother - Davida Goldsworthy....and you have an affinity with gold and gambling.... would you like me to continue?'

Aime pondered her response and then held up her phone showing the picture she had recently received on Facebook. 'Well, you know something about me....I've had my people look into you too. It appears that you have been implicated in a little gold nugget problem in Perth and it is believed that you have left the country – but here you are on my cruise ship trying to convince us to become partners.'

Nic smiled and defensively held up his hands. 'We're not offering a partnership. We only want to borrow some cash, then we'll leave you alone.'

Aime nodded 'So remind me again, what's in it for me?

Rose nodded. 'About three grand. If you help us out, and if I can settle this mess before we leave Sydney, I'll pay you three grand. Easy money. Better odds than the tables.' Aime was still suspicious. 'Do you have anything to offer as collateral? What if you can't settle it before we leave Sydney? Will I get something in return? What if you just take off with my cash?'

Rose tapped at the matchbox, picked it up, and revealed the emerald. 'Only this. I believe you said it was worth around sixty grand.'

Aime smiled. 'Let me think about it. I'll come back at four o'clock and maybe we can make a deal. I might bring Davida with me to convince me otherwise. Perhaps we can have pre-dinner drinks and canapes.' Nic softly tapped her on the shoulder. 'See you then, then.'

Aime turned, left the suite and finally Rose let out her breath. 'Do you think she'll do it?'

Nic nodded. 'I guess we'll find out in a couple of minutes.'

'Don't you mean four o'clock?

'Nup. When I tapped her on the shoulder, I placed a listening bug on it.'

'What if she takes her jacket off?'

'Boy, you ask a lot of questions.'

9

Nic opened an app on his phone, placed it on the table, and they could listen in on Aime's conversation with her bodyguard: *'They are either really stupid or very desperate.'* The man grunted and replied. *'Or there's something else going on. I can't put my finger on it, but it's my gut, and I always trust my gut.'* Aime responded. *'I've seen how much you eat, so I have to agree with you.'*

Their talking became a little muffled and they both laughed. *'I think I'll give them twenty, that will leave us with about ten between me and mum. That should leave enough to put through the tables and convert to chips.'*

Nic and Rose couldn't hear any more conversation, so Rose leaned closer to the phone. 'I think they've stopped talking...what do you think they're doing now?'

Nic leaned back. 'I guess that her jacket has come off. Perhaps it is now on the floor with the rest of their clothes.'

Rose shook her head. 'Let's hope they're getting changed to go for a swim.'

Nic stood up. 'That's one thing I won't be doing.'

Rose nodded. 'Going for a swim?'

'Yep, my face might fall off.'

Rose sighed again. 'So, what are we going to do now? Play hide and no-seek until they come back at four?'

'Nup, I'm off to play shuffleboard. I'm quite good at it you know.'

Rose nodded. 'What? Shuffling or being bored?'

Nic ignored the question. 'Would you like to join me?'

'What if we run into The Hulk and Co?'

'I don't think they're the shuffleboard type.'

Nic and Rose left the suite and headed up to the Entertainment Deck on Level 12 where a game of mini golf was about to commence. Rose noticed there was not a shuffleboard court. 'What a shame, they've done away with the old game.' Nic nodded. 'I guess I'll join in on the golf instead. I'm a good putter too.'

'Is there anything you're not good at?'

Nic grinned. 'I don't think so. Davit Poole is a champion at everything. He's like a real-life James Bond without the cool gadgets.'

Nic moved over to a bucket and selected a putter and a ball. 'Is it too late for me to join in?'

The host nodded. 'No, the more the merrier. This game is closest to the pin. Who wants to go first?' There was a group of players gathered in a huddle and Nic moved forward. 'I will. Which hole are we aiming at?'

'That one.' The hole was half the length of the space on the deck, around thirty metres or so. Rose called out. 'That's one big putt, Davit. Your old skinny arms may not be able to make it that far.' Nic flexed his biceps. 'And I didn't eat my Wheaties this morning.'

Rose responded quickly. 'I'm sure you'll manage, old man.'

The crowd started laughing, and the host called out. 'I love it, heckling from the sidelines already. Come on guys let's make some noise.'

The crowd started cheering and clapping as Nic addressed the ball, drew the putter back and forth a few times, made the putt and the ball skewered off the side of the blade only to hit the foot of a waiter walking past. 'Ouch, try aiming at the hole next time.' The ball ricocheted back onto the artificial grass and stopped about a metre short of the hole. The host called out: 'Good shot, Davit.'

Other players attempted, but no one came close. 'I think we have a winner. Well done. Remember our next competition will be at four o'clock this afternoon.'

Rose leaned forward to Nic. 'You won't be able to make the re-match.'

'Oh well, I think I'm all putted out anyway.'

'You only made one shot.'

'I can't help that. I'm old, but I won, didn't I?

'Yes, I guess. What did you win?'

'This.' Nic held out a small piece of paper. It had "5" on it. 'You accumulate these when you win events on board, then on the last day, you add up all your points and get a prize. I won fifty points on my last cruise and took home a key ring.'

Rose nodded. 'Don't they give them away at the casino on Level 10?'

'I know. How good is that? I can get another one and have matching earrings.'

Rose shook her head and noticed Aime's bodyguard was coming up the stairs behind Nic. He was making heavy work of it. 'I think we'd better go, Aime's bodyguard is coming up the stairs.' Nic turned around, gave the man a little wave and they left the area. Rose looked at Nic. 'Why did you do that?'

'Just to let him know we were still on board. He might've forgotten. I have.'

Rose sighed. 'So, what are we going to do now?'

Nic nodded. 'Why don't you spend some time with the other youngins on board and leave us old folks at the library and the nana-naps?'

Rose looked at her phone. 'It's two in the afternoon. I'm going back to my suite and will ring Mother for an update about Father.'

Nic grinned. 'Remember we have the meeting at four.'

They moved to the lifts, parted ways and Rose headed back to her suite via the stairs. Nic stepped in the lift and pressed Level 10, and Rose assumed he was going to try and get into the private club.

Rose arrived at her suite a few moments later and sat on the couch to call her mother. 'It's me. How is Father?'

'He's very grumpy and not talking to me.'

'That's expected, given the court case over his head. Has Michael turned up yet?'

'He's not grumpy about that. Michael was here this morning and told us he would work everything out. He was looking for that old diary that Father kept in his desk drawer. Do you know where it is?'

'Nope, sorry. Did Michael say why he's looking for it?

'He mentioned something about a password. You know Father can't remember anything, so he writes all his computer passwords in the book. I told him there is an app on your phone for keeping passwords, but he keeps losing his phone too.'

Rose sighed. 'The joys of getting old.'

Jana suddenly took a sharp breath. 'Oh no, your birthday. We missed it. When was it?'

Rose sighed. 'Two days ago.'

'Did you do anything special?'

'Well, I'm on a cruise, sailing from Brisbane to Perth. So, I guess that's special.' Jana went silent. 'Is that man, Nic Thorn with you?'

'He is, but I don't know where he is at the moment, and no, we are not staying in the same suite. I'm on Level 9 and he's in the Honeymoon Suite on Level 5.'

Jana spluttered. 'When did he get married? We didn't get an invitation.'

'He didn't, and we didn't either. It's part of an investigation we are working on.'

'You should be getting married soon, Rosemary, otherwise you'll be left on the shelf.' Rose sighed heavily this time. 'I have been married. You made me do it.'

'That doesn't count Rosemary. I don't know why you keep bringing it up. Anyway, what did you call for? I can hear Father calling out, so I have to go.'

'Nothing really, just checking in. I'll call you in a couple of days when we arrive in Perth.' Rose disconnected and wondered about the missing diary/password issue, so she decided to call Mrs Croud, her parents' ex-housekeeper.

The call was answered: 'Hi Julia, it's Rose.'

'Wow, long time no hear. Where are you?'

'On a cruise about to berth in Sydney. I'm working with Nic on an investigation.'

Julia responded quickly. 'Well, we're only a short drive away, checking into the Newcastle Caravan Park. John is booking a site for a couple of days while we sort out where to go next. I'm waiting for him in the Winnebago. We picked it up a couple of weeks ago. Nic put us onto a guy he knows. Maybe we could catch up if we're that close. It's only a two-hour drive down the coast.'

Rose nodded. 'I think there won't be enough time. We'll arrive in Sydney in the early morning, and we're there just for the day. I don't know if we'll be getting off the boat. It depends on what Nic needs to do.'

'Hug Nic for me, will you? He recommended us to a Financial Planning guy, and he worked out we've got enough to stop working and live the dream. We've been on the road for a couple of weeks and haven't had a single argument.'

Rose smiled. 'Good on you. How did my folks take it that you both left their employment?'

'We haven't told them yet. John is leaving me to make that phone call. I might send a postcard instead. They think we've gone to the Gold Coast for the weekend.'

Rose laughed. 'I've just been speaking to Mother, and she told me Father's diary has gone missing. Would you have any ideas about that?'

'Hold on a minute. Was it the one with the brown leather binding and the map of New Zealand on the cover?'

Rose nodded. 'Wow, that's a great memory.'

'Not really, I've actually got it in my hand. I must have picked it up by mistake when I went through their library gathering my Georgette Heyer collection. I can post it back to them with the postcard if you like.'

'Hold off for a day or two. I'll check with Nic. Mother mentioned a password might be written inside somewhere. It could have something to do with the cryptocurrency fraud charges that Father has been charged with. Can I call you back later this evening?'

'Sure. We'll be here or eating or walking or doing whatever retirees do.'

They disconnected and Rose took a breath, checked the time, located her earbud, put it in, and hoped Nic had his watch turned on. There was no response, so Rose decided to head to the private club to let him know about the recent development.

The lift door to Level 10 opened, and Rose quickly scanned the room, but Nic wasn't there. A hostess stepped forward to hold the doors. 'Back again?' Rose nodded. 'Yes, but I'm only looking for my new friend. He's about yay high and yay round and says yay a lot.'

'He left with a couple of women, something about showing them inside the Honeymoon Suite. Is he on his honeymoon?'

'Yes, but his bride isn't aboard. She gets seasick.'

'Good on him. He's very good-looking, and at his age, he might still find Miss Right.' Rose sighed. 'You mean Miss Right-Now by the sounds of it?'

The hostess smiled. 'Anyway, how can anybody turn down a cruise with us even if they get seasick. We can give them a pill, and it prevents the spill.'

Rose smiled, stepped out of the club, took the stairs down to Level 5, and knocked on Nic's door. It was opened by Aime. 'You're late.'

Rose stepped in, noticed a second woman, and assumed it was Davida Goldsworthy. 'Sorry about that, I had a nana-nap and the alarm on my phone didn't go off.' Nic was serving the drinks. 'Thanks for joining us, Rosalinda. Would you like some champagne?'

Rose shook her head. 'No thanks, I've already had my fill for the day and am feeling a little bloated.' Nic came over, lightly kissed her on the cheek, then whispered into her ear: 'They're on the hook.' Nic stepped back and directed Aime and Davida to sit at the dining room table 'Let's get down to it.'

Nic reached into the bowl of fruit on the table, removed an avocado, sliced it through the middle, separated the two halves and the emerald dropped out. Rose began to rub it clean with a napkin and Davida leaned forward to get a closer look. 'Sixty thousand dollars? You are going to let us keep this until you can get the loan paid back?'

Nic nodded. 'Yes.'

Davida continued. 'What if you don't? Do we get to keep it, or do you track us down and take it from us anyway, and keep the cash?'

Rose added. 'Nope, you'll keep it until we pay you back. I think Davit wouldn't be much of a challenge for your bodyguard if we do anything stupid. He can barely remember to put his teeth in.'

Nic gave a toothless grin. 'So, do we have an agreement?'

Aime took over the conversation. 'Just to get things straight. We hand over the cash; you take it off the ship; pay off the bookie, and then when we get to Perth, you pay us back? Why don't you just get access to your own cash?'

Rose sighed. 'Slight problem with the Banks. I can't get out thirty thousand dollars cash at one time without them filling out one of those stupid Suspect Transaction Reports, so I have to withdraw it in small increments. I can get some at our next stop, then Melbourne, Adelaide, and finally in Perth.'

Davida and Aime huddled together, and then Aime looked at Rose. 'OK, we're in, give us a moment to get the cash organised. We'll be back in twenty.'

About half an hour later the doorbell rang, and Rose stepped up to the peephole. 'It's Aime's bodyguard, and it looks like he's alone.' Rose opened the door, and the man grunted. He then moved to the coffee table, dropped a leather backpack on it, looked at Nic, and held out his hand. 'Give me the stone.'

Nic handed him the avocado. The man squeezed it into a pulpy mass, dropped the squished green fruit on the floor, stepped on it, and then leaned down to gather the emerald. He put the stone in his mouth and sucked the avocado residual from it, then put it into his pocket. 'Money in bag. See you in Perth.' The man then left the room leaving the door open.

Nic opened the backpack, turned the backpack upside down and two rolls of cash tumbled out. 'It looks like we got at least twenty.'

Rose took a breath. 'That was a bit easier than I thought, but I do have a question how are we going to come up with twenty thousand dollars cash, surely we can't just give them the same bundles back, it may look a little suspicious.'

Nic shrugged. 'Plan C.'

Rose sighed, moved over to the bar fridge, removed a small bottle of non-alcoholic gin, cracked it open, took a swig, and sat down on the couch.

'I needed that. Oh, by the way, I spoke to Mother, apparently Michael in is a bit of a tizzy as he can't find Father's diary, she mentioned something about a logon and password being written inside it.'

Nic smiled. 'I bet he is.' Rose continued. 'So, I rang Julia to see if she knew anything about it. They're staying in Newcastle, and we might be able to meet up with them if we go onshore.' Nic nodded 'Interesting.'

'Oh, no...that's not the interesting bit, Julia has the diary.' Nic smiled. 'Well, that sounds like a plan. I'll call it Plan D.' Rose shook her head. 'You're going to run out of letters of the alphabet. What's Plan D?'

'How do you feel if I got off the ship in Sydney and flew to Perth? I've been speaking to Chewy about the missing gold and it sounds like the investigating Detectives have got a strong lead. We have been asked to get over there ASAP.'

Rose sighed. 'How are *we* going to get off? Surely, Aime will get suspicious?'

'Well, *we* may have been diagnosed with COVID, and *we* may have to be quarantined to my suite for the protection of the other passengers and jump ship, and that means *we* can avoid being seen until *we* can get back onboard in Perth.'

Rose looked at him. 'Both of us? I don't think that will work. You're expecting me to move from my suite? I like my suite and don't think I want to stay in yours...with you...in the Honeymoon Suite.'

Nic considered his options. 'OK, how about Plan E? When we meet up with Julia and John to collect the diary. Do you think they might like to come on board and stay in the Honeymoon Suite? You can stay on board with them.' Rose nodded. 'I like the sound of Plan E,' so she called Julia and they arranged to meet in Newcastle.

10

The cruise ship sailed overnight to Sydney, and after breakfast, Nic and Rose disembarked, made their way through the security checkpoint and were collected by a driver who drove them up to Newcastle. Nic had stashed the cash into his passport wallet, so they headed to the local Commonwealth Bank to put the money into a Safety Deposit box. The receptionist looked up his name and box details. 'You haven't been in here for a while, Mr Poole.' Rose held her breath, wondering if Nic had ever been in the Bank.

Nic smiled. 'No, I believe the last day was the 28 December 2019, on the thirtieth anniversary of the earthquake. What a spectacle that was.' The bank officer nodded. 'Yes, quite. Oh, it looks like we need to update your identification.' Nic smiled. 'Sure, I have an electronic driver's licence, will that be OK?'

Rose leaned forward and managed to read the name. "Davit Poole".

'Thank you Davit. I'll have one of the staff members process that while we are downstairs in the Safety Deposit Area.'

Nic and the attendant then headed to the Safety Box vault and returned ten minutes later. Nic nodded at Rose as he reached the top of the stairs. 'Thank you, I hope it doesn't take another earthquake for me to return to Newcastle.'

The bank officer nodded. 'I'll keep that in mind and hope to see you back soon.'

While she was waiting, Rose had taken the time to write down some thoughts about what to tell John and Julia. They left the Bank and looked around for a suitable site to meet with up with them and settled on a coffee shop, sat down and Rose ordered lunch. 'They're meeting us at one, so we have some time to go over the plan.'

Nic nodded. 'There's not much to tell them. They'll be quarantined in the Honeymoon Suite until they arrive in Perth. Hopefully, no one bothers them.'

'OK, that makes sense, but I've got some other concerns. Apart from getting them back onboard.' Rose pulled a small notebook from her handbag and leafed to the appropriate page. Nic grinned. 'Hit me baby, one more time, or twice or three times. How many times is up to you, and what you hit me with.'

'Well, what happens if Aime does discover you're no longer on board? John and Julia might be able to hide, but surely they can't be expected not to enjoy the benefits of being on a cruise.'

Nic smiled. 'John only needs to get on board with the mask, then he can remove it once he's in the cabin, otherwise, they'll be free to move around the ship.' Rose looked at him. 'Hang on, if he takes the mask off, he won't be able to leave the cabin, and I assume his name is now Davit Poole?'

'The cruise cards don't have photo ID, only the cabin number, so as long as he does it carefully, he'll be right.' Rose shook her head again. 'But Julia is supposed to be married to a guy that looks a little like the movie actor guy, not some other guy pretending to be that guy.'

Nic shrugged. 'Boy, your questions make sense sometimes.'

Rose sighed. 'It's my job, and speaking of jobs, you'll have to take that mask off before John and Julia arrive.' Nic nodded. 'I can't.'

Rose shook her head.' We've been over this before. You can and you will.'

'But don't laugh when I return. I still don't have any head hair or eyebrows.' Nic stood up, headed to the bathroom, and returned a few minutes later. He had a red bandanna wrapped around his head and had drawn eyebrows on with a black pen.

Rose tried her best not to laugh. 'You look like a pirate. Oh, and I thought of something else. What are we going to do about getting the money back to Aime when we arrive in Perth?'

'Nothing.'

Rose put her head into her hands. 'OK...tell me why?'

'Because we're not going to meet them, and they won't want to find us.'

'Where will we be?'

'In jail.' Rose shook her head again. 'I don't want to know anymore.'

Nic laughed. 'You asked.'

It was now nearing one o'clock. Rose took another sip of her coffee and looked up. 'Here they come. They look ten years younger.' Rose stood, they hugged, and she directed them to sit down.

Nic shook their hands. 'Good to see you guys, and thanks for coming. Are you settled in at the caravan park?' Julia smiled. 'We're at The Big 4, Newcastle Beach. It's not that far to drive.'

Rose nodded. 'How do you manage that? We didn't mean you have to come down in the Winnebago.' John smiled. 'We use a Mini Cooper Countryman when we're not driving the big bus. It slips into a space built into the rear of the van. Nic sorted that stuff for us too.'

Nic shrugged. 'Yep, I find stuff, do stuff and sometimes I know people with stuff.'

John continued: 'You often see the big rigs with the little cars in tow, so we went one better and got a rig with car storage in the rear. It makes more sense. Anyway, what have you guys been up to?'

Rose smiled. 'Living my version of the dream, but it's turning out to be a little bit of a nightmare. We're in the middle of an investigation and it's getting a bit nasty. Nic might explain some more about it, but we'd like to ask a favour.'

Nic leaned down, picked up the briefcase, and placed it on the table. 'There's something in here that is going to be exciting and a little dangerous.'

John leaned forward. 'You'd like us to join you in an investigation? Rose has filled us in a little of what you two get up to with the scam-busting things but never mentioned you might need some help. Are these our disguises?'

Rose shook her head. 'Not quite. It could still be dangerous.'

Julia smiled. 'That sounds even better.'

Nic clicked open the briefcase to reveal a squished silicon head mask. 'Actually, it's a couple of things. Firstly, how would you like to cruise from Sydney to Perth, and secondly, John, are you allergic to silicon?'

John grinned. 'You want me to pretend I'm someone else?'

'Not quite, well sort of, but it depends on whether you guys want to do it.'

Rose nodded. 'I'll still be on board the cruise ship with you, but you two might be confined to your suite as you both have COVID.' Julia smiled. 'We've had all our shots.' It then dawned on her they were expected to board the cruise ship. 'You mean right now?'

Rose nodded again. 'Yes, Nic has been requested to get over to Perth ASAP, for an update on the investigation into some missing gold. So, we were wondering if you'd like to take his place on the cruise ship and then fly back here after that.'

Julia looked at the crumpled face. 'Where's my mask?' Rose continued: 'You don't need one as you will be playing the role of a new wife who doesn't like cruising but decided to join her new husband on your honeymoon.'

Julia nodded. 'Does that mean we're in the Honeymoon Suite?'

Nic shrugged. 'Yep.'

John finally caught up with the conversation. 'So, you want me to put on a mask, pretend I'm someone else, and we both have to stay hidden for four days on a cruise ship, staying in the Honeymoon Suite because we have COVID. Then, when we arrive in Perth, we fly back here and continue as if nothing happened?'

Rose sighed. 'That's about it. Did I mention you'll have a butler?'

John smiled again. 'So, what's the dangerous bit?' Nic took over. 'There are a couple of people on board that we owe some money to. I won't go into it yet, and I think they're going to get a little annoyed if they find out I'm no longer on board.' Julia smiled. 'But Rose will still be.'

'Yep, but it's Rosalinda, and she is your clients ex-wife, and John, your name is Davit Poole.' Julia nodded. 'It's all rather confusing. If John is Davit Poole, am I Mrs Poole?' Nic continued. 'Not quite, you'll still be Julia Croud. John won't have to wear the mask in the suite as long as no one comes in. Our first task will be getting you back on board without raising suspicion.'

Nic re-opened the case and removed two cruise cards - neither card had a name, just the suite number. 'These are your cruise cards. Your portraits have been uploaded to their database. They might be pleased to see you as I told them my new wife gets seasick and wasn't joining me, but you changed your mind.'

John nodded. 'So, the biggest challenge will be getting back on board. I've done a bit of acting in my younger days. I'm sure I can come up with something. Do I need to put on an accent or anything like that?'

Rose shook her head. 'Nope, you are playing a grumpy, dopey guy in his mid-seventies. Nic has been playing the role for a few days, you'll be fine.'

Nic went quiet momentarily. 'I think I'll fit you out in a leg-cast and arm brace, that way you won't need to say anything as you'll be in too much pain after your accident.'

John smiled. 'What accident? Do I need to have a quick lesson in being hit by a car? Tuck and roll, tuck and roll.'

Rose nodded. 'Nope. It might just make it easier to get past them if you're in a wheelchair and can't stand up. I think you're a couple of centimetres shorter than Nic. We've got a couple of hours to work on it as we're due back on board at four.'

John stood up. 'OK, we'll see you at the cruise terminal about four.' Rose shook her head. 'Sorry, not quite. Julia will need to get a suitcase organised, then will try the mask on and go over the story a few more times. How long did you book in for at the caravan park?'

'Just a few days.'

'OK, we'll cancel the booking, and if it's OK with you, Nic will drive the Winnebago down to Sydney and put it in storage until you return from Perth. There's a place at Epping we've used before; it will be safe there. If you have any expenses, just keep the receipts and we'll reimburse you.'

Nic nodded. 'I love it when a plan comes together.'

Rose shook her head. 'Plan, what plan? We're making this up as we go along.'

Nic smiled. 'That's part of the plan.'

The group moved out of the café, returned to Newcastle, and entered the Winnebago. Julia filled a suitcase, and John showed Nic around the vehicle and how their car was stored in the back. 'It's like driving a whale, just remember to allow extra space for everything.' Nic nodded. 'I've driven one before, it was up near Broken Hill but there wasn't that much traffic. Rose can tell you about that scam-busting story later.'

They returned inside and found Rose referring to her notes. 'Do you have any questions? You can still walk away.' John looked at Rose. 'They say retirement is an adventure. What a way to start.'

Rose sighed. 'It's not going to be that easy. There's a lot that could go wrong, even at the first hurdle of getting back on board, but I'll be there to keep things on the lowdown.'

Nic went to stand and bumped his head on the air conditioning unit, so he removed the bandana to check if there was any damage. There weren't any. John looked at him. 'When did you go bald, and what's with your eyebrows? It looks like you drew them on.' Nic grinned. 'Oops, sorry I may have forgotten that you may have to shave all the hair from your head to fit the mask on.'

Rose nodded. 'And of course, there's the other thing.' Nic grinned. 'Oh, shaving your eyebrows...well that's up to you.'

Rose sighed. 'I'm talking about the diary.'

Julia smiled and held up the diary. 'I was wondering when you'd get to that. I flicked through it and would say your father has written most of the details and passwords in it for all his banking and other stuff.'

Julia went to hand the book to Nic, but Rose intercepted it mid-pass. 'There might be personal stuff in it about me, so how about I look through it first and let you know if I can let you read it.'

Nic shrugged. 'I wonder if he's written anything about me.' Rose shook her head. 'It's not big enough.'

Rose leafed through the pages and stopped at the letter P. 'He's listed the passwords under P for password so that it makes it easier to follow.' Rose then went to the front of the book and looked under C. 'The login details and account numbers are under each letter. This one is C for Cryptocurrency, so then you flick to P and find the password. Simple. It's not in Father's writing though.'

Nic shook his head. 'No wonder Michael wants the diary.'

Meantime, John had flattened his hair, put on the mask, settled it onto his head and as the mouth was in place, he managed to lick his lips. 'My head is a little smaller than yours, so I'll look even more wrinkly. Anyway, what is this scam-busting fraud thing all about?'

Nic put the bandana back on. 'Let me quote you the famous words of Stalag 13's Sergeant Schultz: "I know nothing."'

John grinned. 'So, if I'm bailed up by someone onboard, I use that?' Rose looked over to Nic, he nodded, so she continued: 'Maybe, but I doubt we'll run into them, as they're in the possession of a very large and very fake emerald.'

Julia looked at her. 'How do you know it's fake?'

'Because we gave it to them. I'll fill you in a bit more once we're on board.'

Julia smiled. 'So that's why they're angry with you?' Nic shook his head. 'They don't know it's fake and they won't know it's fake unless someone tells them.' John rolled his head a few more times to settle into the mask. 'OK, let's get this show on the road. Let's find a leg brace, put on the arm sling, drop me into a wheelchair and I'll practice looking old and grumpy.'

Rose smiled. 'You won't have to work hard, Nic has been wearing it for the last two days and his expression never changed.'

Nic shrugged, and they returned to the car to drive back to the cruise ship.

11

Nic directed John to stop the car about three hundred metres from the cruise terminal, and they went into a mobility assistance store to collect the wheelchair, the arm sling, and the leg brace. Rose handed over her credit card for the rental and gave the receipt to Nic. 'Here, file this please.'

Nic took a photo with his watch, balled up the docket, and tossed it towards the nearest rubbish bin. John smiled as best he could through the silicon mask as the paper ball had missed the bin, bounced off the wall, and rolled back to Nic's feet.

'I'll get it.' John picked up the paper ball, put it into his pocket then looked at Nic's watch. 'I didn't know they could take photos too.'

Nic shrugged. 'It can't. I just wanted to take the basketball shot. Let's get you kitted out with these things. I think if you make grumbling noises, wince in pain, and ignore any sympathy offered, we might just pull it off. I'd better head off and will see you in Perth.'

Nic moved towards Rose, and it appeared like he was about to kiss her on the cheek, so Rose drew her head back. 'Hey, watch it.'

Nic shook his head. 'I was just going to get the earbud back. You won't need it.'

Rose removed the unit and placed it in her handbag. 'I think I'll keep it with me, thanks all the same.' Nic nodded, saluted, and walked away. 'Good luck then, I'll call you later to check how it went.' They watched him get into the car and Rose sighed. 'Well, let's get this show on the road or the ship as the case may be.'

The trio were heading towards the cruise gate when Rose suddenly stopped. 'Wait here, I've just had a thought.' Rose guided Julia to a seat, withdrew her phone from her handbag, moved off to make a phone call and five minutes later she returned. 'OK, I've just heard that the cruise ship is having computer issues and it's likely that we'll be waiting at least an hour to get back on board.'

Julia nodded and stood up. 'Did they ring you?'

'Nope, I rang Chewy, and he made it happen.'

Julia looked at her. 'Why?'

'Because I realised if Chewy can upload your portrait to get you on board, why couldn't he upload John's headshot? That way we don't have to go through all of this mask malarky. Chewy needs about half an hour to finalise it, so let's go back to the mobility store and return all the stuff.'

John smiled, removed the leg brace and arm sling, and then headed into a restroom to remove the silicon mask.

A few minutes later, they were standing at the counter of the shop. John handed over the arm sling and the salesperson reviewed the crumpled receipt. 'How long ago did you rent the chair?'

John nodded. 'About half an hour. My niece paid for it on her credit card. Check the records. You wouldn't have had that many wheelchairs, leg braces, and arm slings rented in the last twenty minutes, then being returned.'

The salesperson looked at the receipt again. 'Why is it so crumpled?' John continued. 'My mate balled it up and tried to throw it in the bin, he missed, so I picked it up. Luckily, I didn't throw it away.'

'So, where is he? I thought there were four of you.' John stammered for a response and Rose stepped forward. 'He's driving to Sydney.' The salesman nodded. 'OK, but where is the man that needed the wheelchair?'

Rose responded quickly. 'We've already put him on board the cruise ship. They provided us with one of theirs, so that's why we're returning yours.'

The man thought about the comment. 'That makes sense, but why are you returning the arm sling and the leg brace?'

Rose smiled. 'Because he got better.'

The man shrugged; the EFTPOS machine went "Bing" and spat out the receipt for the refund. 'I've refunded in full, but next time, please make sure you need them before getting better.'

Rose nodded and took John's arm; then the trio left the store and headed to the cruise terminal. Julia took a breath. 'That was close. You were pretty quick to come up with a response.'

Rose shrugged. 'I've been working with Nic for a while now, and I've learned to be prepared for any wrinkles in the plans.' John nodded. 'I guess that's why you've changed the plan to get on the ship,'

'Yes. It didn't make sense to stop you from enjoying an all-expense paid cruise to Perth by hiding in your rooms.' Julia smiled. 'What did he say when you told him you'd changed the plan?'

Rose shrugged. 'I haven't, but Chewy will update him.' Julia nodded again. 'We haven't met Chewy. How does he fit into all of this?' Rose smiled. 'He's our go-to computer guy and lives in Melbourne, but we don't let him into the field very much as he likes to arm himself with a plastic Star Wars lightsaber, whereas Nic likes to use his wits instead. Fewer batteries to replace.'

John grinned. 'Star Wars, Chewy. He's the big woolly pilot of the Millenium Falcon.' Rose nodded. 'So, I've heard. I've only watched the first two, which I think were the third and fourth ones. They're up to number twelve now. Maybe they'll have them showing on the cruise ship. It's my only hope.'

The trio joined the queue to return to the cruise ship and John was getting a little anxious and whispered to Rose. 'Are you sure this is going to work? How did you get our details uploaded so quickly? What happens if we can't get on?'

'Don't worry about it. Just enjoy the cruise. We'll take care of it.' Rose helped them load their suitcases onto the conveyor belt to be scanned and they collected them on the other side. Julia let out her breath. 'That was easy.'

Rose winced. 'That was the easy bit. The next part is getting onto the ship. That's where they'll check the cruise cards against your cabin details. It might get a bit tense, but please remain calm whatever happens.'

John whispered. 'Are you expecting trouble?'

'I guess we'll find out.'

The queue for the cruise ship's gangway had stalled so Rose moved out of line to find out what the delay was and returned to them. 'They're trialling a facial recognition system, so you won't need your cards. Luckily you took off the mask.'

John shrugged. 'If I didn't come off the boat, how will I get back on board?'

'Simple. You've both joined the cruise here in Sydney. Remember, if it all gets too uncomfortable, you can disembark in Melbourne.'

Julia sighed. 'Nic has thought of everything.'

'Nope, this is all me. Nic was staying in the Honeymoon suite, but I don't think that will work as I'd like you two to have a lower profile. I've arranged to relocate the couple that were in the suite next to me to his cabin. You two are now next to me on Level 9.' John nodded. 'Why would they move?'

'They're on their Honeymoon.'

It was finally their turn to pass through the security. Rose went first and waited for the others. 'Welcome back Miss Jardin.' John then stepped up to the camera, and nothing happened. 'Please step back sir, you're too close.' John took a breath and stepped back, but still nothing happened. 'Do you have your cruise card, Sir?'

Rose managed to get a glimpse of the screen, but the image was black. It occurred to her that they might not have waited long enough for Chewy to upload the new image. A senior security officer moved closer to them. 'Sorry, what seems to be the problem?'

'This man's image is not on the screen. It's someone else. Same name but....' The steward looked at John, then looked at the image. 'Are you just joining us or were you onboard?' John was fumbling for his cruise card when the computer screen went blank and the lights went out in the small area. John stepped back and whispered to Rose. 'Wow, do you think Chewy blew the fuses?'

Rose shook her head. 'He is clever, but I don't think so.'

The security officer looked at John. 'Please wait here sir as it looks like we may have a slight problem with your identification.'

Rose quietly considered if it was a delay in Chewy's making, but her concerns were allayed as the security officer stepped forward and handed over the cruise card. 'Sorry for the delay Mr Croud, welcome aboard.'

The Officer then announced to the others waiting in the queue: 'Cruise passes and ID only. Please have them ready. Our facial recognition system is down at the moment. We depart port in an hour, but I assure you we will have you all onboard.'

Julia held up her cruise card and used her Driver's License for ID. The trio then caught the elevator to Level 9 and Rose led John and Julia into her cabin.

12

Twenty minutes later, the doorbell rang, Rose opened it, and Leyla was standing there. 'Hi Rosalinda, are you sure this is OK? Rocky considered booking the Honeymoon Suite, but we decided it was way too expensive. Surely, we owe you something for the difference?'

Rose shook her head. 'Nope, you're doing me a favour. My friend was staying there by himself as his new wife didn't like cruising, so he decided not to continue. Please enjoy the experience. Oh, and if anyone asked what happened to him, just tell them you don't know anything.'

Leyla nodded. 'Should I be expecting someone to ask?'

'No, but you never know what goes on aboard these ships. Loose lips sink ships and all that. Anyway, have you shifted all your luggage yet? I've also managed to find another couple to take over your cabin.'

'Yes, the cabin steward organised all of that. Thanks again Rosalinda. Let's keep in touch.' Leyla hugged Rose and headed off.

Rose closed the door. 'You can come out now John and Julia. Your cabin is ready.'

They moved out of Rose's cabin and entered the one next door. 'Welcome to Mansion Suite No. 8.' Julia smiled. 'Wow, this is how the other half lives.' John chuckled. 'We're the other half now, Julia. I could get used to this.'

Rose opened the bar fridge. It was fully stocked with high-end alcohol. 'And you can have any drink you want; there's no expense spared, so please enjoy.'

Julia shrugged. 'Not much good for us. Neither of us touch that stuff anymore. We've had to clean up too many after-parties at your parents' place.'

Rose pulled out a small bottle of chardonnay and cracked open the top. 'Sorry about that. Well, it looks like I'll have to drink by myself. "Cheers". Speaking of my parents, have you told them yet?'

John looked a little sheepish. 'Not yet, perhaps you can.'

Rose nodded. 'Leave it with me. Speaking of my parents again, when did you decide you'd have enough money to take the plunge into retirement?' Julia smiled. 'I think it was when we hit half a million each in our super funds amongst other things.' Rose grinned. 'Wow, how did that happen?'

John nodded. 'Your father did a lot of business in the back of his car, and I spent a lot of time driving him around.' Julia smiled. 'And I picked up other investment opportunities when I was cleaning his home office. A couple of months ago I overheard Michael talking to him about investing in Bitcoin. We put five grand in and when it recently peaked, we cashed it in and it helped to buy the Winnebago. I can see why Michael wants to get his hands on the diary.'

John took over. 'I overheard he's got at least two million in there, and if it crashes, he has a lot of explaining to do. The Tax Department did legitimise it as an investment in 2017, but it still scares a lot of people, and they wouldn't be happy if they find out he's been putting all the investments just in your father's name.'

Rose nodded. 'So that's the link.'

John sat down. 'What can we do to help?'

'Well, firstly you have to keep a low profile, and don't mention you know me, Nic or Davit Poole.' Julia moved over to the bar and poured a mineral water. 'You mentioned someone we have to avoid. Do you have a photo of them?'

Rose moved to the escritoire, opened the top drawer and removed the portraits of the two women. 'This is Amethyst Davey, she calls herself Aime, and this is her mother, Davida Goldsworthy, and there are over two thousand people on board so hopefully you don't run into them.'

Julia took the photographs. 'Which one of them has the fake emerald?'

'Aime, and she also has a bodyguard. We named him Hulk. I assume she keeps him around as she's carrying bags of cash which she has been converting to casino chips. She's the one that we sort of borrowed twenty thousand dollars from to pay off a gambling debt.'

'Sort of?'

'Yes, we sort of made up a story about me having to ante up some funds to pay off my ex-husband's gambling debt, and handed over the fake emerald as collateral.'

Julia was shocked. 'Michael has started gambling again?'

Rose smiled. 'This has nothing to do with Michael. It's part of the ruse, the set-up. We use backstories to gain people's confidence as it helps us control the investigations. In this case, I'm a recent divorcee, and my ex handed over a bunch of money when the settlement went through.'

Julia shook her head. 'I still don't understand why your Father thought it was a good idea to marry you off. Anyway, it's water under the bridge as they say, maybe one day you'll find the love of your life and settle down.'

Rose shrugged and took a sip of the chardonnay. 'I'm settled, it's just that I live in a constant state of continuous excitement working with Nic.'

John moved over to Julia and took the portraits from her. 'Can we keep these?'

'Sure, but don't let anybody see you have them.'

Rose put the chardonnay down. 'I'm going to my cabin to change into something more comfortable. I'll see you for dinner at six.' John shook his head. 'No, you won't. We don't know you.' Rose nodded. 'Good. The first test passed. I won't see you for dinner or hopefully anywhere on board the ship.' Rose stepped out of their cabin and returned to hers.

Julia began to sort the luggage and store it away. 'This is our first cruise, and hopefully the first of many more. Did you know a Cruise Specialist is on board and we qualify for major concessions as we're in a Mansion Suite?' John smiled. 'I know. She's on Level 5 and I've already made an appointment at seven o'clock tomorrow night.' Julia nodded. 'When did you do that?'

'On the television, while you were talking to Rose.'

'Well done. So where are we eating tonight?'

'Cabria Restaurant. It's Italian, and we've got a booking at 5.30. I did that on the television too.' Julia smiled. 'Is there anything else on the television worth seeing?'

'Nope, and as far as I'm concerned there's only dust. We're not going to waste our time staring at the idiot box. It's about time we started talking to other people.'

Julia grinned. 'So, what's our backstory?'

'We're an old married couple spending their twilight years cruising around the world.'

Julia shook her head. 'Really? Is that all you could come up with? How about we're a couple of retired spies enjoying our last hurrah? Or better yet, we're a couple of high rollers that have been banned from every casino around the world, and we're going out with a bang on board this ship that has unlimited gambling opportunities on Level 10.'

John grinned, picked up the two photographs and tossed them onto the bed. 'You know, there's a hole in your plan.' Julia shrugged. 'What's that?' John grinned again. 'We don't know how to gamble at cards or craps or whatever they have on board here. Besides, Rose asked us not to go to Level 10 in case we ran into Aime and Co. Let's just say we're a recently retired couple from Brisbane that used to manage a property.'

Julia nodded. 'Kiss.' John moved forward and lightly kissed her on the cheek and she stepped back. 'What was that for?' John shrugged. 'You said kiss.' Julia shrugged. 'I did, but it means; Keep It Simple Stupid, but I'll take a smooch any day of the week, and here's to happy cruising.'

They were dressed for dinner an hour later and were about to leave when the doorbell rang. Julia went to the peephole and peered through. 'Are we expecting anyone? There's a mountain of a man standing outside our door.'

John shrugged. 'Maybe it's Rocky, he might have forgotten something.'

Julia opened the door. 'Hi, can I help you?' The man looked into the cabin and nodded to John. John returned the greeting. 'Rocky?' The man moved from side to side with the ship's motion. 'Yep, rocky.' Julia stepped back, allowing him to enter and John continued. 'Have you forgotten something?' The man smiled, then noticed the portraits on the bed, moved over and picked them up. 'Why do you have photographs of Aime and Davida on your bed?'

Rose had been standing on her balcony, moved inside to make a phone call and three thousand kilometres away in Perth, Nic's phone rang. 'Yep.'

'I'm ringing to let you know Plan F worked.'

'F? I didn't get to F. I stopped at E. How come you went ahead without me?'

'Take a guess.'

'You decided to have Chewy upload John's ID after he had added Julia, then you returned the wheelchair and stuff. John removed the mask, and you boarded the ship without any worries.'

'Not quite.'

'Did I miss something?'

'Nope, but I got Chewy to upload his details after returning the wheelchair, which was way before we boarded the ship.'

'Semantics. Apart from relocating Rocky and Leyla to the Honeymoon Suite, and putting the two J's into their suite, what else was in Plan F?'

'You've been speaking to Chewy.'

'Yep, and Nup. The cruise company rang me to find out why I left the ship.'

'What did you tell them?'

'I said that a nasty lady in one of the Mansion Suites was harassing me so much I just couldn't stay on board.'

'Was that when you were Nicolai Epine or Davit Poole?'

'Not sure, but she managed to chase both of them off the ship.'

'Nic, can you be serious, please? I'm keeping the two J's on the down-low, so now they're able to enjoy the cruise. I'll try to avoid Aime and Davida, and Hulk, and hopefully, they'll not notice that you're not aboard.'

'Gee, that's a good plan. Let's call that Plan G, for good plan.' Rose sighed. 'Let's call it Plan G for good grief. So, what's the latest with the gold? Do I need to jump ship in Melbourne, and fly over to join you in Perth?'

Nic went quiet. 'Not sure yet. I've got a meeting in the morning with the Head Detective. It was quite embarrassing for the Perth Mint to lose a batch of bullion, and a few people have egg on their faces. Actually, that makes sense, as the middle bit of the egg is yellow, and I'm not yolking.'

Rose sighed. 'What's the time over there?'

'We're three hours behind you. So, I've got some catching up to do if I want to keep up.' Rose sighed again. 'Goodbye Nic, and say goodbye to Nicolai and Davit for me as well.'

Rose disconnected, stepped back onto the balcony for some sea air and could overhear a conversation in the next suite. Julia was speaking loudly: 'I don't know who they are. The pictures were on the bed when we arrived. The couple that were in this suite have moved somewhere else. We don't know anything.' A man's voice responded. 'I'll leave you alone then.' John made the next statement. 'Who are you and why did you come into our suite?'

Rose assumed the man had ignored the question and that he had left the cabin as she heard a door shut in the passage.

John and Julia then came together, hugged each other and Julia stepped back. 'Should we call Rose?' John shrugged. 'I don't know but there wasn't much room here with the three of us.'

Julia sighed. 'Well, I'm going to call Rose and let her know about that little visit by the very big man.' Julia pressed the room number and Rose answered quickly. 'Hi Julia, I overheard. Who was he?'

Julia continued 'I know we're not supposed to know anything, but he was a very large man. He saw the pictures of Aime and the other woman and wanted answers.'

Rose grimaced. 'What did you tell him?'

John responded. 'Nothing,' I said we'd only just joined the cruise. We don't know anything.'

Rose sighed. 'Good. Next question. What did he look like? I've met Aime's bodyguard, but not Rocky Mountain. He's Leyla's husband.'

Julia was about to respond when their doorbell chimed again. John moved to the peephole and looked through, then turned to face Julia. 'It's looks like the Aime woman. What should we do?'

Rose overheard the comment and took a moment to consider what was about to happen. Julia held the phone closer to her ear. 'Did you hear that, Rose? Are you still there?'

Rose responded quickly: 'Grab the photos off the bed and put them into the safe. Give it a moment, open the door, but don't let her in yet. Leave the phone off the hook.'

Julia took a breath. 'I'm coming, give me a sec to tidy up.' She collected the photos, put them into the safe and nodded at John to open the door.'

John slowly pulled down the handle. 'Hello, are you from housekeeping?' Aime remained where she was. 'No, I'm …. I'm looking for someone. They told me they were in this suite.' Julia was gripping the phone and called out 'We've just boarded. We don't know anything about anything. I'm on the phone with housekeeping as we want softer pillows and an extra blanket.'

Aime took a long look around the suite. 'Do you know what happened to the guests that were staying in this suite?' Both John and Julia shook their heads and Aime continued. 'Apparently, they're on their honeymoon.'

John nodded. 'Did you try the honeymoon suite? Maybe they went there.'

Aime nodded slowly. 'OK, I'll leave you to it then.' John closed the door, leaned against it and let out a long breath. 'I think this adventure is way outside our comfort zone.'

Julia picked up the phone. 'Are you still there? Did you get all that?'

Rose nodded. 'Yes. I'm so sorry it's all getting a bit ugly. This is what can happen sometimes.'

Julia nodded. 'What should we do now?

'Order room service and get housekeeping to deliver the blanket and extra pillows. I'll track Aime down and hopefully find out what she knows about things. Hopefully, she hasn't realised Nic has left the ship. Leave it with me and please try to enjoy the cruise. Don't let this get in the way of having a good time.'

John called out. 'I think we'll get off in Melbourne. Will that be OK?'

'Yes, sure. I'll organise plane tickets back to Sydney and we'll have the Winnebago delivered to the airport for you.'

Julia sighed. 'You don't mind? We'll pay you back.'

'Nope, it's all good. Just lay low until we get there.'

They disconnected and Rose thought about calling Nic, then decided to call Chewy instead to have him organise the change of plans. Rose rang but the phone went to a message. "Call me. Change of plans." A couple of minutes later Rose's phone rang. It was Nic. 'What's the change of plans?'

Rose sighed. 'Is Chewy there with you?'

'Yep.' Rose then overheard a Wookie woofing sound in the background. 'Tell him I've watched another one of those Starry War films and as far as I know, Chewy never speaks until he's spoken to.' Nic nodded. 'But he gets so excited when he hears your voice. What's the change?' Rose explained about the recent visit that the two J's had to endure and confirmed arrangements would be made to have them leave the ship at Melbourne.

Nic went quiet for a moment. 'Has Aime realised I'm AWOL?'

'No idea, I haven't caught up with her yet. I'll head off to Level 10 after this call and see what's what. If anything, I'll remind her that she shouldn't be anywhere near me or my cabin, at least until we dock in Perth.'

'OK. See you then.'

Rose hesitated. 'What do I tell Aime and Co if they realise that you're not here?'

'Tell her I'm on board somewhere but we're not talking as we had a heated discussion about your ex-husband's settlement. He wants some money back.'

'It's at least three days until we get to Perth.'

'Yep, then tell her I'm really good at hide and seek.'

Rose shook her head and disconnected.

13

In a borrowed office at Perth Police Headquarters, Nic and Chewy were finalising their plans for the next stage of the investigation. Nic opened his phone. 'I'll call Elvis to see if he can help out again. He has access to planes, trains and automobiles, so that should do the trick.'

Chewy nodded. 'I assume Aime took the bait with that photo I uploaded?'

Nic nodded. 'Yep, hook, line and sinker. That photo was quite a good mock-up, but Rose knew it wasn't me dressed in the mask. I didn't tell her it was you.' Nic made the call, and it was answered promptly: 'You've rung Elvis. Are you lonesome tonight?'

'Hey mate, where are you?'

'In Freemantle, just leaving a 7-11. Hang on, let me put my deep-fried PB&J sandwich down. What's up?'

'Are you available to fly us around for the next week or so?'

EIGHT DAVE'S ARE WEAK – 133

'For you, I'll make it work. Are Sandy and Rose with you?'

'Nup, not yet. Chewy is here with me, but Rose is on a cruise heading here and Sandy will join us here soon too.'

'I hear you, Nic. Will you need a two-seater like the one in the photo or something larger?' Nic nodded. 'Larger, as it has to be able to fly over long distances and land in the scrub.'

Elvis went quiet for a moment. 'I can get access to a Black Hawk or a Bell Long Ranger, both of them will seat about six people plus gear, but the Black Hawk comes with machine guns.'

Nic laughed. 'I don't think we'll need the Black Hawk.'

'When do you need it by?'

'Monday next week. Chewy and I have a meeting tomorrow with the lead detectives on something, and we have to wait for Rose and Sandy to arrive.'

Elvis nodded. 'OK. Leave it with me.'

They disconnected and Chewy folded out a map of Western Australia. 'It's a long way to the MacDonnell Ranges from here. It looks like about two and a half thousand kilometres, which is about thirty hours by helicopter. I don't think it's going to work. We'll need to take a commercial flight to land in Alice Springs and find something to drive us out there. It's just over an hour's drive.'

Nic smiled. 'Yep, I've thought about that already. QANTAS flies from Perth to Alice Springs every three days and from Adelaide every day, so Sandy could meet us there. I'll can get Elvis to have a chopper on stand-by, and we'll can rent a couple of Four-Wheel Drives from Alice Springs.'

Chewy nodded. 'I know a guy.' Nic smiled. 'I thought you might. I'll ring Sandy to find out if she wants to join us.'

Nic made the call and Sandy quickly answered in a whispered tone. 'Hi Nic, what's up?'

Nic remained cheerful. 'Where are you? How's your Dad?'

'He's taken a turn for the worse so I'm back at the Royal Adelaide Hospital.'

'I'm so sorry, Sandy. He's strong and will pull through.'

'I know, but this COVID thing has taken a lot of people down. I caught it again even though I've had three shots. I hope I didn't give it back to him. What's happening?'

'I was going to ask you to meet us in Alice Springs. We're looking into a missing gold thing, but it sounds like you've got your hands full there.'

'Yes, I have. I might have to skip this one. I skipped the last one too and the time before that when Rose sorted out the Mildura missing car thing without me.'

Nic smiled. 'I think you're going to need another skipping rope. Take care of him and yourself, and we'll bring you back in when he's better.'

'Thanks, Nic. Oh, and please remind Rose to stay away from you.'

'Easy, peasy. I'm in Perth and she's on a cruise ship somewhere east of Sydney.'

They disconnected and Nic decided to ring Rose to update her on things. The call connected. 'Hey, it's me.' Rose whispered into the phone. 'Yes, I know but I'll keep it low. I'm in the dining hall and this place has a lot of ears.'

Nic responded quickly. 'Will do, are they serving corn on the cob again?'

Rose ignored the comment. 'I think Aime has got wind that you aren't on board.' Nic nodded. 'Me or Davit or Nicolai?' Rose sighed. 'I don't think she cares who it is. I've seen Hulk scurrying around with a determined look on his face as if he's searching for you. Aime can't be far behind.'

'Does John still have the mask?'

'Yes, why what are you thinking?'

'It's about time you have some company, and she sees you with Davit Poole. Just update him on the lawyer/ex-husband thing and have him meet you for dinner.'

Rose considered her reply. 'Julia is onboard as John's wife and now you want her to be seen with someone else?'

'Yep, just put an upside-down pineapple on their cabin door.'

Rose went quiet momentarily. 'What's that supposed to mean? Oh, no, I'm not doing that.'

Nic laughed. 'Well, make something else up. Just keep it simple.'

'OK, will do. I have to go. I just saw his Hulk-i-ness coming this way. I think he's doing another sweep.' Nic laughed. 'Or wanting something else to eat.'

'He's already been through here twice and each time grabbed a plate full of food.'

'Only twice. Well, in that case, he must be starving. Poor guy.'

'I'm hanging up now, unless there's anything else.'

'Nup, apart from Sandy won't be joining us to look into the gold thing. Her Dad is still crook with the COVID thing.'

Rose sighed. 'That's a bad thing, and a good thing then.'

'Which is which, Rose?'

'I think you can guess. I'm going now. I'll see you in Perth or will I be joining you in jail?'

Nic nodded. 'Neither, as it might be Alice Springs. I don't quite know which one yet.'

Rose closed the call and considered how to best manage the shifting situation on the cruise ship. Half an hour later, after searching aft, bow, port, starboard, and everywhere else boaty, Rose finally located the two J's in a private spa area. They were the only occupants.

Julia peeled off an avocado facial mask, then raised her champagne flute. 'Welcome to The Spa. My name is Julia, and the man under the other mask is my husband, John...but it could also be Davit.'

Rose closed the door behind her. 'Well, this time I'm Rose. I think John needs to put his Davit Poole mask on. We're going to have to act out a charade to placate Aime and her marauding Hulk. I think they're getting a bit edgy, given Davit Poole appears to have gone AWOL.'

John sat up and peeled his facemask down. 'Why? Do they suspect something?'

'Not sure, but his Hulk-i-ness has been marching around the place looking for him. Davit Poole might have to make an appearance to lower the anxiety levels.'

John nodded. 'So how do you want to do this?'

'We'll use the sick bay suite. It's on Level 2. Put the mask on, grab the ice bucket, pretend to throw up into it a couple of times. I'll meet you there in an hour and don't be surprised if Hulk or Aime is with me.'

Julia nodded. 'What do you want me to do?'

'Stay in your cabin. It will be easier that way.'

14

John and Julia headed back to their cabin, and Rose began her search for Aime & Co, eventually finding them on Level 10. Aime was handing over cash and replacing them with chips, not bothering to play any of the tables. An older woman was sitting with her and Rose realised it was Davida Goldsworthy, so she quietly moved beside them. 'Hello, Aime. Have you been looking for me?'

Aime kept staring forward. 'We're not supposed to be talking to each other. Why are you here?' Rose sighed. 'I've seen your Hulk-man stomping around the ship. It's quite obvious he's looking for someone.'

Aime momentarily stopped shovelling the gambling chips into her handbag. 'I'm not talking about it here. Come with me.' Aime stood up, beckoned Hulk to join them, and they headed to a small room where a foursome was playing mahjong. Aime stepped into the room and looked at them. 'Get out.'

The group stopped playing and Hulk collected the tiles, put them back into the box and "helped" them move out of the room. They didn't care to challenge him.

Aime then held up her hand, indicating to Hulk that he was to stay outside. Rose sat down but Aime and Davida remained standing. Both women began to pace around the small space, and eventually, Aime stopped. 'I don't know what scam you are pulling here but Davit Poole, your friendly neighbourhood gold scammer, appears to have disappeared. Has he left the ship?'

Rose carefully considered her response realising Aime must have re-watched the Facebook post. 'I have no idea. What does it matter?'

'Because it does. He, or you, have twenty grand of ours and we want to know if we're going to get it back.'

Rose took a breath. 'I assume he's still on board somewhere. I haven't seen him since we made the arrangement. That's what's supposed to happen.'

'I don't trust him, or you for that matter. We want our money back.'

'I can't do that Aime, you know that. We're in the middle of the ocean. I paid my guy off in Sydney. You'll get your money when we get to Perth. Besides, you still have the emerald.'

Aime sighed. 'And we still don't like it. So, I tell you what, my big friend here will be joining you while you both search the ship for your little lawyer friend. We've seen that Facebook post. What was that all about?'

Rose shrugged. 'I've no idea what you are talking about.'

Aime sighed heavily this time, then rapped on the door, and the large man joined them in the room. 'You and Rosalinda are going on a treasure hunt. Don't stop until you find the elusive Davit Poole. We'll be waiting here.'

Rose stood up. 'Fine. Whatever. We'll start on Level 1 and won't stop until we drop. He's here somewhere. I've seen him around, but we're not supposed to be looking out for each other.'

Hulk escorted Rose to the nearest escalator, and he pressed '1', but nothing happened. Rose pressed it again. 'Looks like Level 1 is staff only.' The man nodded, but said nothing, so Rose added. 'We'll go to Level 2 and take the stairs down.'

Hulk took a small notebook from his back pocket and finally spoke in a low gravelly voice. 'He was in the Honeymoon Suite. Another couple in there now.'

They arrived at Level 2, stepped out, and moved towards the stairs. 'Why is Aime so anxious to know where he is?' Hulk shook his massive head. 'Not him, she's anxious because you took the cash and stopped us from converting them to gambling chips. I'm not saying anything more so don't ask.'

'Sorry, I do have one more question.'

The man glared at Rose. 'You are very annoying.' Rose continued. 'What did Aime mean about seeing the Facebook post?' Hulk stopped on the stairs between the flights. 'It was about a gold nugget. Your lawyer friend has been trying to sell a gold nugget that he found.'

Rose nodded. 'Oh, that. I've heard about it. It's ancient history. No one is taking it seriously as it's too big to have been undiscovered for so long and has raised a few eyebrows around the place. They are waiting for the test result to confirm how pure it is. I don't know him that well. He was my ex-husband's lawyer, not mine.' The Hulk-man grunted. 'Don't care, but Aime does. Gold is her thing. No more questions, lady.'

They reached Level 1, where the large internal doors on both sides read "Staff Only". Hulk grunted again. 'Find someone to let us look around.' He then moved toward the nearest door and started thumping his fist on the panel. 'Open up. Open up.' There was no response. Rose checked for the time on her phone. 'Let's try Level 2 and come back down if we have to.'

They ascended the stairs, and Rose headed towards the Medical Centre. 'I'll ask if they have any patients.' Rose rang the bell on the reception desk, and a woman in a white laboratory coat appeared from behind them. She was wearing a full PPE shield and a blue N95 face mask. Rose realised it was Julia. The "Doctor" moved to the other side of the desk. 'Can I help you?'

Hulk took over the conversation. 'Do you have any patients here?'

'Yes, but under the Doctor-patient privilege, we cannot discuss the matter unless you are a direct relative.'

A gurgling noise came from a consulting room behind the doctor. The door was closed, and it was labelled "Under Quarantine."

Hulk decided to ignore the doctor's comment and the door warning. 'I'm going in there. Get out of my way.' He pulled open the door, stepped into the room and the sound of a man retching split the silence.

Hulk yelled out 'Found him,' and quickly retreated from the room covered head to toe with a copious amount of vomit. He stormed off to find the nearest bathroom to clean himself up and remove the creamy stream of viscous fluid dripping from his clothes. The "Doctor" called out after him. 'It's the worst case of emesis we've had on board for a long time. The stench will stay with you for days.'

Rose allowed herself to smile. 'It does stink. What was it?'

Julia raised the PPE shield and lowered her mask. 'A mixture of oatmeal, tapioca pudding, and mashed potatoes. I took a spoonful of each from the dining room and mixed them in the bucket on the way down. I think my work here is done.'

John then exited the room and began removing the "Davit" mask. 'I guess he's gone. I think I managed to get it all over him. I used the whole bucket.'

Rose smiled. 'Good job, but it wasn't exactly what I had in mind. Anyway, I think you'd better get out of here before a real doctor turns up or the Hulk comes back.'

John nodded. 'The doctor is attending an emergency. I called it in. There is only one doctor and one nurse on board at the moment. Another team is joining the cruise in Melbourne.'

Rose nodded. 'How do you know that?'

Julia smiled. 'I overheard that the others remained in Sydney on sick leave, so we decided to set this up. Apparently, there is a case of bad flu on board this ship.'

About twenty minutes later, up on Level 10, a very grumpy, damp, and stinky Hulk hustled his way through the casino area to find Aime and Davida still sitting in the small room. He angrily pulled open the door. 'I found him. He's still on board. In the sick bay.'

Aime nodded then noted the man had quite an unpleasant air. 'You stink. Get out and get cleaned up.'

Hulk took a large sniff of his clothes. 'I've already showered twice. I can't get the stench out of my hair. He threw up on me. It was definitely him.'

Aime laughed. 'That's fully sick, bro.'

15

In Perth, Nic was conducting a meeting with the Detectives on the case. The matter of the suspect gold nugget had been raised. Nic nodded at Chewy. 'It's part of the plan to get the suspected perpetrators interested in the gold. An anonymous post was made to Ms. Davey's Facebook site, and we are about to upload details as to where the nugget was located. We believe the gold their group obtained is being stored near the MacDonnell Ranges, west of Alice Springs, which incidentally is where my nugget was found. My team will be heading there directly to undertake further investigations.'

One of the detectives referred to her notes and put her hand up. 'I'm Senior Detective Kelleigh Brook. I assume you're aware that the Cross Border Justice Scheme allows us to investigate the matter in the Northern Territory?'

Nic nodded. 'Yes, I am.'

'Interesting. So why is your team investigating the theft of the gold?'

'We would appreciate any assistance. However, I have been advised that your resources are stretched given the Heads of Government meetings are underway here in Perth.'

The Detective nodded. 'That's attended to by local and Federal Police, not us.'

A Senior Officer interrupted their discussion. 'Acknowledged Detective Brook, but please let Mr Thorn update us on his investigation and then we'll discuss the matter of allocating additional resources. Please continue, Mr Thorn.'

Nic nodded. 'Our investigation has uncovered two parts of the crime. The first is the stolen Bank Cheque allegedly used to purchase the gold bullion. That matter is being handled internally by the Bank involved. The second part is the shipment of the gold, and the use of the aeroplane to transport it to the site where we believe the gold is currently located. Detective Phelan can elaborate on that matter.'

Another Detective stood up. 'We believe they loaded the gold onto a Saab 340 which they flew from the Jandakot Airport to Alice Springs, stopping to refuel twice. CCTV shows evidence of a fuel purchase, made in cash, at the Kalgoorlie Airport. The second refuelling stop is not known at this stage. We have yet to locate the whereabouts of the pilot.'

Nic moved toward and flipped over a whiteboard. It showed portraits of Amethyst Davey and Davida Goldsworthy and a picture of Hulk, but no name was shown. There was a fourth black square. It read "Pilot?"

Nic continued. 'At this stage, we do not know who the pilot was or in fact, if he is involved in the heist, or an innocent bystander. We believe not all the gold was put onto the plane due to the weight and remains somewhere in Perth to be melted down and or converted into cash.'

Detective Brook stood up and moved to the whiteboard. 'There are not many people here that could assist with the conversion of such an amount of gold, and we are using our networks to try and locate them.'

The Detective hesitated then looked at Nic. 'I can add the name to your un-sub pilot. I believe his name is Dafydd Barkel. He has been operating a helicopter service for tourists between Perth and Rottnest Island. The business is under investigation due to an alleged case of gross negligence. A passenger fell from an open-sided helicopter into the sea during one of the crossings. Fortunately, she survived, but Dafydd Barkel's flying days may be over.'

Chewy leaned forward and whispered to Nic. 'He is Elvis's business partner. He was allegedly doing unsafe maneuvers.'

Nic whispered back. 'I didn't know. It changes things.' Nic re-addressed the group. 'Thank you for the update, Detective Brook. I'm sorry, but at this stage, we are unable to continue with the presentation. We may have a conflict of interest. One of my associates jointly operated the helicopter business. Can we please reconvene once I have discussed the matter with him?'

The Senior Officer looked at Nic. 'We will give you twenty-four hours. Please bear in mind that your team may be removed from any further investigations into this matter.'

Nic nodded. 'Chewy can you pack up? I've got to have a little talk with Elvis.'

Chewy began to remove the items from the whiteboard and box them up. 'Elvis should be out the front waiting for us.'

Nic went through the Police Headquarters, located Elvis at a coffee shop, sat down, and took a breath. 'Tell me about Dafydd Barkel.'

Elvis looked at Nic. 'Who is that?'

Nic sighed. 'Your mate that pilots the helicopters.'

'His name is Dafydd Barkel? I've only ever known him as "Debacle."

Nic shook his head. 'He dropped someone from his helicopter.'

'Right, that. Well, we had a falling out. I've not seen him for months.'

'You mean you had a falling out as the passenger had fallen out?'

Elvis smiled at Nic's statement. 'True. I've had to shut the business down until her legal people talk to my insurance people. I have a mediation session tomorrow. I thought that's why you were in Perth to support me.'

'No, we're here investigating a gold heist from the Perth Mint, and now I find out it could indirectly involve one of my associates. It's not a good look.'

Elvis nodded. 'Since when has not having a good look ever stopped you from investigating stuff? All of your investigations were about not having a good look.'

Nic smiled. 'Yep, but that was always from the other side, not my side. Do you know where he is and whether he's involved in the relocating the gold from Perth to Alice Springs?'

'How much gold?'

'About four hundred gold ingots - five thousand kilograms, which is roughly worth a million dollars. They used a Saab 340 to transport it across the states.'

Elvis let out a whistle. 'That's a lot of gold and would likely be too heavy for the Saab. How did they get it to the airport without anyone noticing?' Nic tapped on his phone, and it brought up a picture of a white Toyota HiAce van. 'With this.'

Elvis leaned forward to get a closer look. 'So, is the gold still in Alice Springs airport?'

'Nup, it appears that had a similar vehicle waiting there when they arrived. It was last seen heading south along the Dukes Highway, and believed to be somewhere out near the MacDonnell Ranges.'

'That's a large area to search.'

Nic smiled. 'Yep.'

Chewy arrived, and he was shaking his head. 'They've given us until five tomorrow afternoon to sort this out. We need to get back to the Hotel and debrief.'

Nic stood up, but Elvis didn't move. 'Sorry about all this. Give me half an hour to check a few things out and I'll catch up. Are you staying at the Westin in Hay Street?' Nic nodded. 'Yep, and we'll be in one of their meeting rooms on the ground floor when you've finished. See you then.'

The dynamic duo headed to the Hotel, while Elvis walked to his car. He sat inside and began scrolling through his phone. 'Just what have you got yourself into, Debacle?' He found his contact number and rang it. It went to message. *'You know who this is, now tell me who you are. Leave a message.'* Elvis sighed. 'Not going to work, buddy.' He called another number, and this time it was answered.

'What do you want?'

'Where is he, Connie?'

'How the hell would I know? I haven't seen him for weeks. My girls want to know, too. They're too young to understand what is going on. What do I tell them? Are you ringing to tell me he's dead? Otherwise, I told you not to contact me.'

Elvis sighed. 'I just need to find him. The mediation is tomorrow, and if he doesn't turn up, I could lose everything.'

'Like I care. You sacked him without even hearing his side of the story. We have nothing now. I've had to sell the car and the boat, and some deadbeat is trying to talk me down to buy the jet-ski. I don't want to deal with this crap.'

'He dropped her from the helicopter, Connie. There's the vision of him skylarking. She could've been killed.'

Connie quickly rebutted his comment. 'She fell into three metres of water. It wasn't that deep, and the helicopter wasn't that high.' Elvis sighed again. 'I'm sorry that you have to go through all of this, but my business is about to be wound up, and I have to limit my liability. You're welcome to join me tomorrow at the mediation.'

Connie went quiet for a moment and responded in a softer tone. 'Look, I don't know where he is and don't know if he's coming back. This is the new normal for me now. I don't know if...' Elvis hesitated. 'I can send you some more money. I still have your banking details. Would that help?'

'Thanks...it would. I have to go. If I hear from him, I'll let you know.'

'OK, that would be good. Remember, tomorrow, ten o'clock, at the Laab Lawyers Office, 533 Hay Street. It would be good if you could make it.'

Elvis closed the call and considered who to contact next but decided to take the half-hour drive to the Jandakot Airport instead. This is where their business was based. He was waved through security and parked in the hangar in front of the three Robinson Helicopters. It was the smaller, two-seater R22 Bell II that Debacle had been flying the day he dropped the passenger. Normally, they would use the larger Bell Ranger 206, which could take up to seven passengers, however, both of them had been loaned to the Perth Fire Brigade to do aerial surveillance on that fateful day.

Elvis tapped the bulbous front windscreen of the little R22 unit. 'I'm sorry, little one, I'm going to have to let you go. I hope I can find you a nice new home.'

The helicopter had blue police tape across the open doors as it had been declared a crime scene. Elvis leaned in to look at the dashcam that he had specially installed to capture the passenger's special moments and wondered if anything had been filmed. The unit had to be carefully removed to avoid damaging the windscreen, so he doubted anyone had bothered to check. He went over to the tool chest to collect the modified tool he had specifically made for the task, but couldn't locate it, so he decided to use a bevel-headed screwdriver. Elvis then considered whether he would be legally permitted to remove the unit, so he rang Nic. 'Any news, Nic?'

'Nup. Chewy and I are working through this gold thing. Did you find him?'

'No, but that's not why I'm ringing. It's about collecting evidence.'

'What do you need to know? You can't take anything that can be used as evidence; only the police can do that. I blur the lines occasionally but have never crossed them deliberately. What's up?'

'I'm at the hangar. I installed a dashcam on the R22 and want to check if there was any recording of the event. The vision is saved onto a data chip. I don't think anyone has checked if it's still in there. The little helicopters only have an E.M.U. which just records the engine information. No voice or vision is available.'

Nic considered the response. 'Why haven't you done this before?'

Elvis hesitated. 'The helicopter has police crime tape on it. I just didn't think of it. I thought Debacle would turn up, and it would all get sorted.'

'Do you think he would have removed it?'

Elvis hesitated again. 'I don't know. It's quite a tricky process to get the thing off the window without it breaking or damaging the window. I doubt he would have known how or even bothered.'

'OK, let me make a call, and I'll ring you back. Don't do anything just yet.'

Nic disconnected, and around twenty minutes later, he called back. 'You have the permission to remove it, but make sure you take pictures on your phone of everything you do. It would be better if you had a witness. Is there anybody else around?' Elvis nodded. 'I can find someone.'

'Good, do that. Make sure that they are independent of your business.'

'Will do, Nic. Sorry for all of this.'

'Good luck and let me know if you find anything.'

They disconnected, and Elvis went searching for his witness. Fortunately, as the security guard was on a break, she was happy to assist. Elvis brought her back to the hangar, explained the situation, then set his phone to video, pressed record, and handed it to the guard. 'I have the approval to remove the dashcam from the windscreen bracket to check if the computer chip is still inside. You may be called as a witness for the mediation meeting tomorrow. Are you OK with that?'

The guard nodded. 'Yes, and for the record my name is Tristesse Church, I am a security guard at Jandakot Airport. I am an independent witness to what is about to transpire on this day, Thursday, the 7th of March, at 10 a.m. I am in the presence of Aron "Elvis" Preslin. He is the owner-operator of the helicopter.'

Elvis took a moment to process what the guard had just said. 'You sound like you have done this before?' Tristesse nodded. 'I am a J.P. in my other life.'

Elvis smiled, raised the police tape, stepped into the cabin, and sat in the passenger seat. 'I'm unclipping the dashcam from the bracket on the windscreen.' He began to jimmy the box from the bracket, the plastic box yielded, and he looked at Tristesse. 'That was much easier than I expected. I am now removing the unit from the cabin and carrying it to my work desk.'

The guard followed Elvis and stood next to him at the desk. Elvis turned the unit over, located the eject button for the chip, and pressed it, but nothing happened. Tristesse leaned forward. 'It looks like it's been removed. Do you concur?'

Elvis wiped his brow with his hand. 'I do. Thanks for your help, I'm sorry to have wasted your time.' Tristesse nodded. 'Well, it was a good idea. Maybe your business partner took it.'

Elvis sighed. 'Or maybe the passenger took it, or it fell out, or was never in there in the first place.' Elvis waited for the guard to leave, then called Nic. 'It's me again.'

'Any luck?'

'No, but the chip has to be somewhere. I always put one in, but maybe it fell out.' Nic nodded. 'Or maybe he took it, or could the passenger have taken it?'

Elvis sighed again. 'It doesn't matter now. Whatever happens tomorrow happens, it's just....' Nic waited for Elvis to continue. 'Just what?'

'Just everything...it's the end.'

'No, it's not Elvis, it's a bump in the road. I'll help you buy a steam roller and you can flatten it down.'

Elvis smiled. 'Thanks, Nic. Are you coming tomorrow?'

'Yep. Ten a.m. See you then.'

Nic disconnected and looked at Chewy. 'Do you think they'll give us any more time?'

Chewy shook his head. 'I had to beg for twenty-four hours. I don't think they want us to do this one. It looks like they are embarrassed by the breach of their security protocols.'

'Yep, that's what I was thinking too. Did you manage to put together the route the HiAce took from the Perth Mint to the airport?'

'Yes. I'm just waiting for my AI programme to patch it together. It will send me an SMS when it's done.' Nic smiled 'If only I could get my coffee machine to know when I need a caffeine fix. That should be something AI could be working on. It's getting late, and we have a big day tomorrow, let's finish up and start afresh in the morning.'

Chewy nodded. 'Good idea.'

16

At six a.m., the following morning, Nic was waiting for Chewy in the breakfast bistro. Chewy entered, sat down, and set up his laptop when his phone chimed. 'It's here.' Nic nodded. That was quick.' Chewy smiled. 'Not really, I'd been working on it all night. That, along with the flight tracker. I've found the plane. It's still in Alice Springs.'

'Why haven't the police found it?'

'I guess they haven't got around to it. I'll call the airport a bit later.

'Anything else?'

'Nope, but I think we'd better find a private room to watch this. It could put the Perth Mint Security Team and the police in a compromising position if anyone else sees it.'

The duo was about to relocate to one of the empty conference rooms when Nic noticed Elvis standing at the reception desk. 'Elvis is here. I wonder if he's found something. He knows the local streets. It would be good for him to see it.'

Chewy went into a conference room and began plugging things in and setting things up while Nic approached Elvis. 'Morning mate, you look like death warmed up. Haven't you slept?' Elvis shrugged, and Nic continued. 'We're about to watch the route the HiAce took, then we're going to have breakfast. Care to join us?' He shrugged again, and they made their way over to Chewy.

Nic closed the door behind him and Elvis took a seat. 'I couldn't sleep. In four hours, I find out if I still have a business to run. I don't know what's next for me.'

Nic smiled. 'You could work for me full time, you know. I could use a pilot on standby, but you might have to leave the West and head over to the East.'

'Thanks, Nic. I guess something will come up.'

Chewy had finished linking his computer to the projector, rolled down the screen, and closed the curtains. 'This was taken on the 1st of March, the day of the heist, and starts at the Perth Mint. We can follow them via various street cameras along the route. There's only an overhead of them collecting the bullion, so you can't see anybody's faces.' He pressed "enter" and the vision began. It showed two people loading the gold into the HiAce, and snippets of a third person in the driver's seat.

Nic nodded to Chewy to pause it. 'So, there were three. It looks like the big guy is Hulk. I met him on the cruise ship and the second one looks like Aime. I can't quite see the driver but suspect it's Davida Goldsworthy.'

The group finished loading the gold and the woman climbed into the passenger side, while the man stepped into the vehicle's rear. Chewy moved toward the screen. 'The van should be easy to follow. It has a heavy-duty luggage rack on the roof and added a dual wheel axle. They would have needed to reinforce the chassis to carry the gold.'

Elvis leaned forward. 'Well, that's not Debacle driving, which I guess is a good thing. When he's not flying, he always wears a West Coast Eagles cap on backward.' Chewy pressed enter and the vision started again.

The van drove out of the CBD, over The Narrows bridge, along Highway 2, through South Perth, and eventually turn left into Jandakot Airport. The patchworked vision lasted for fifteen minutes, and then the screen went blank.

Nic sat back in the chair. 'Nothing out of the ordinary. They were lucky with the traffic, kept under the speed limit, and didn't draw attention to themselves. It was well planned and executed.'

Elvis shook his head. 'What a joke. They turn up with a dodgy Bank Cheque, collect a million dollars of gold, and drive away. It's that easy.'

Nic nodded. 'Yep, the planning, the stealing of the Bank Cheque, driving to the airport, all without being caught was the easy bit, but disposing of four hundred ingots of gold is going to take some effort. We're already on to them and I assume they'd need a specialist gold trader, one who won't ask any questions to convert it into cash. Gold is useless as a commodity as you can't go to the local supermarket to buy your groceries, and it has to be stored somewhere.'

Elvis allowed himself to smile. 'And they say crime doesn't pay.'

Nic nodded. 'It does sometimes, but only in cash.'

Chewy closed down the van vision and brought up a PowerPoint presentation showing various scenarios, situations, and sites. 'I worked on this on the flight over from Melbourne. It's my version of Jenga, and when we pull out the last piece it will all fall on top of them.'

Elvis nodded. 'You haven't added Debacle's name as the pilot, is that a mistake?'

Nic smiled. 'Nup. We're going to leave his name out of it until we work out exactly how he fits in it. We don't have any evidence that he's directly involved, and he might just be an innocent bystander who flew the plane under duress.'

Elvis nodded again. 'Well, he's guilty of something otherwise he'd still be here somewhere. Can we shut this down and have breakfast? I don't want to go to this meeting on an empty stomach.'

Chewy closed things down, wrapped things up and the trio went to breakfast.

It was nearing ten o'clock. Nic and Elvis were sitting outside the lawyer's conference room waiting to be called in for the meeting. Elvis checked the time on his phone for the umpteenth time and felt resigned that Connie would not be joining them. 'She's not coming, Nic.'

'She'll be here mate. Chewy has gone to collect her, and that's the good news.'

'What's the bad news? They called and are not going to make it?'

'Nup. She's bringing her kids with her.'

The elevator chimed, the doors opened and a frazzled Chewy stepped out. He was holding the hand of a two-year-old and his other hand was pushing a pram. Connie stepped out from behind him. 'Sorry, we're late. We had to change a nappy. Your friend here is quite a master at it, yet he has no children. He did mention something about wrangling computer cables though.'

Chewy let go of the child's hand and the tot ran up to hug Elvis. Elvis leaned down and tweaked her nose. 'Hey, little one. You get bigger every day.' The girl squirmed at the response and returned to her mother. Connie was introduced to Nic, and they all took a seat outside the conference room to wait.

It was now five minutes after ten and there had not been any movement from inside the meeting room. Elvis checked the time on his phone again. 'Perhaps they've forgotten?' The door opened and a legal-eagle-type man stepped out. 'Parties for the mediation. Please follow me inside.'

The awesome foursome, with two children in tow, stepped into the room where it was wall-to-wall legal eagles. Nic directed his team to sit down, but they couldn't decide where as there were at least twenty chairs around a massive bespoke walnut table. They ended up sitting opposite each other well away from the six legals sitting at the other end. Connie put her daughter onto her lap.

One of the legal eagles stood up. 'I am Selwyn Laab, you may have noticed my name on the door,' he chortled at his comment and continued: 'Thank you all for coming today. I see you have brought along your own representation, Mr Preslin.'

Elvis shook his head. 'No Sir, I haven't. This is my friend, Nic Thorn, he is a Private Investigator, and his associate, Chewy. This is Connie, Debacle's wife, Oh, and these are their kids. They are here for moral support.'

Laab smiled knowingly. 'Well, we still recommend you have representation. Who told you that you didn't need it.'

Elvis lowered his head. 'You did.'

Laab nodded. 'Be that as it may, do you wish to continue?'

Nic held up his phone. 'I can have a lawyer here within a few minutes should you wish to wait. He mentioned he could be available. His name is The Honourable Justice Davood Meddles, perhaps you've heard of him?'

Laab glared at Nic, then changed his expression and looked over at his team. 'I don't think we'll need to bother The Honorable Judge at this time. It's only the first of many mediation meetings, thank you for the offer though. Please, let us continue.'

Laab sat down, and another lawyer stood up, moved to the front of the room, and handed a loose-leafed folio to Elvis. 'We have prepared a summary of the matter and would like the defendant to confirm the details.'

Elvis began to read the brief, and then Connie put her hand up. 'Sorry, where is the other party? I thought that both parties need to be present during a mediation.'

Laab scoffed. 'No, they don't. They can elect a representative, and that's me.'

Nic put his hand up this time. 'Be that as it may, I believe that we are entitled to see a copy of the undertaking appointing you as her representative. It is called a "Notification of Representative Commencing or Ceasing to Act", Form 11.'

Another one of the legals scrambled to locate the form and held it up for Laab to collect. 'I believe this is the aforementioned form, Mr Thorn.' Nic put his hand up again. 'Can I see it please?'

'No, you may not. It is for court-appointed persons only.'

Nic put his hand down. 'Fair enough. Sorry, I just need to send a text, please continue.' Nic tapped at his phone and a few moments later there was a knock on the door, and he stood up. 'Excuse me, I believe that will be for me.'

Nic opened the door and a distinguished man stepped in. He walked over to Selwyn Laab to shake his hand. 'Good to see you again old man, how are the twins?' The man then addressed the group. 'Apologies for my tardiness, and for those that don't know me, I'm The Honourable Justice Davood Meddles.' The man then sat down next to Connie, and she gave him a peck on the cheek. 'Thanks for coming, Dad.'

Laab sat down, chewed at his bottom lip for a little bit of courage, took a deep breath, and nodded at the lawyer at the front of the room for her to continue. 'The matter at hand involves our client being ejected from a two-seater Robinson Helicopter due to the negligence of the pilot. We note that the pilot, Dafydd Barkel is not present today and at this stage, the representative of the business, Mr Aron "Elvis" Preslin, is in attendance. We will proceed after we take a short break. Coffee will be served in the kitchen to the left as you exit. There is water available here in the room.'

Connie leaned toward her father. 'That was quick. It must be thirsty work being a lawyer.' Davood grinned, 'And it just cost her about a thousand dollars.'

The litany of Laab lawyers left the room so Nic moved over to Davood to formally introduce himself. 'Nic Thorn, nice to meet you, Sir.' Davood nodded. 'Finally, a face to a name. Elvis has told me so much about your team and I know of that wine scammer and reptile smuggler you brought down in Margaret River a while back. Quite a reputation you have, Mr Thorn.'

Nic nodded. 'It's not just me. I have the support of a small working team and have guys like Elvis around Australia that help me out when needed.'

Davood was about to respond when there was a wail from one of the children, as she had pulled the dashcam unit from a bag that Elvis had brought into the meeting. Connie was trying to wrestle it from her. 'Please let it go, Arya. It's not a toy.'

The child continued to cry, but Chewy had managed to remove it from her grasp by substituting it with a small wooden horse that he had purloined from one of the bookcases. 'Horsey wants to play, neigh, neigh. Horsey wants to play.'

The child took the horse and began to canter around the room. Chewy let out a breath. 'I'm used to dealing with dungeons and dragons, not children.'

The dashcam unit was otherwise undamaged and Chewy was setting it on the table just as the litany of Laab lawyers returned. Laab noticed it. 'So, is this the dashcam I was called about?' Elvis nodded. 'Yes, it is but it's empty. The chip is missing.' Laab smiled. 'Oh, what a shame.'

Connie pushed it forward to remove it from the grasping hands of her daughter. 'It's not a shame. That's why we're here. Can we get on with it please?'

Laab nodded and looked at Elvis. 'On the basis that I permitted you to extract it from the helicopter, I now wish to see the video taken with your phone to ensure it was not tampered with.'

Chewy gathered his laptop, stood up, and hooked it to their wall projector, then pressed play. The vision and audio were clear and confirmed that Elvis had not tampered with the unit before discovering the chip was missing.

Elvis whispered. 'I couldn't find the tool that I normally use so I used the screwdriver instead. What a waste of time that was.'

Nic picked up the unit. 'Not exactly. Chewy can you please replay the part where Elvis is climbing into the cockpit.'

Laab looked at him. 'To what end?'

'Please bear with me.'

Chewy replayed the vision and it showed Elvis sitting in the passenger side seat and attempting to pry the unit from the screen. It finally snapped out of the bracket. Nic called out 'Stop. Now we can all see that Elvis is sitting on the passenger side, and he is removing the unit with the screwdriver. It has caused rectangular gouge marks on the left-hand side of both the back and the left flank.' Nic held up the dashcam to show everyone and Laab nodded. 'So what?'

Nic continued. 'So, why are rounded gouge marks on the right-hand side and the back? It appears that someone may have removed it previously, using a different type of tool, similar to this one.'

Nic again held up the unit to reveal the second set of tool marks along the right-hand side. He then nodded to Chewy, and a photograph of a modified metal crochet needle was shown on the screen. It was about ten centimetres long and had an enlarged hooked tip.

'Chewy can you please focus the vision to the right-hand side of the windscreen bracket now that the dashcam unit has been removed?'

Chewy rolled the mouse and the close-up showed evidence of tool marks on the pilot's seat side of the windscreen and Nic continued: 'To leave those scrapings, we could assume that someone sitting in the pilot seat has used a tool similar to this one, perhaps to remove the chip and then returned the unit back it into place.'

Laab scoffed again. 'That doesn't mean anything, and why would they do that?

Davood stood up. 'Actually Selwyn, it raises the element of doubt that the unit may have been tampered with, and the chip removed by persons unknown. It is sufficient to suspend any further mediation until the matter is fully investigated. Do you concur?'

Laab was slow to respond so Davood continued: 'Furthermore, as the legal representative in absentia, it is within my power to appoint Nic Thorn as lead investigator on this matter. There will be no further correspondence with my client until I am satisfied with the outcome. Please direct any such queries to my office.'

Nic stood up and gestured to the others to do the same. 'I think we can go now, thank you for your time today, Mr Laab. We will be in touch.'

Elvis, Nic, Chewy, Davood, Connie, Arya, the little wooden horsey, and Sansa, the infant in the pram, then left the lawyer's office to find a place to debrief. They settled on the Westin Hotel. It was a ten-minute walk. The group gathered around a large table and Nic shook Davood's hand again. 'You stole my thunder.'

Davood nodded. 'I was wondering what you had discovered. So, are you available to work point on this investigation?'

Nic nodded. 'Yep, we're actually here investigating the theft of gold bullion and it appears Debacle may be involved. He flew a plane containing the gold from Jandakot Airport to Alice Springs. Whether under duress or not, we're not sure.'

Davood smiled. 'Yes, Connie told me. If you need anything, just let me know.'

Chewy stepped forward. 'Actually Sir, we met with the Detectives yesterday about our case, and due to the relationship between Elvis and Debacle, we were given twenty-four hours to justify our continuance of the investigation.'

Davood nodded. 'Task Force Niffler I believe. Detective Kelleigh Brook is the lead. Leave it with me.' Nic nodded. 'Thank you.'

'I may not be able to get an extension, but I could have a word to them about her joining your investigation. Would that be a suitable alternative?'

Nic smiled. 'I hope she likes working in the outback, as we're heading to Alice Springs A.S.A.P.'

17

Back on the cruise ship, Rose was standing on the top deck watching passengers disembark. The ship had sailed overnight into Melbourne, and day trippers had been given a couple of hours of free time to explore the city. Rose opened her phone, stared at the photo of Debacle, and wondered how she could manage to get it in front of Aime & Co. Rose whispered 'Damn, you, Nic.'

It then occurred to her how it might just work, so she scrolled through her phone and stopped on the selfie that Nic had taken in the singles bar of herself, "Nicolai" and Aime. 'Hello, Nicolai Epine. Where have you been hiding all my life?'

Rose selected the photo, emailed it to Chewy, and then rang Nic. 'Hey, it's me.'

Nic responded. 'Hi me, you must be missing me.'

'Actually, it's Nicolai Epine that I'm missing. I just emailed the selfie you took of me, you, and Aime in the bar. Do you think Chewy could edit you out of it and replace your image with Debacle? I'll use it to find out what Aime knows about him.'

Nic nodded. 'Makes sense, good idea. He'll have it back to you in a jiffy.'

Rose nodded. 'Speaking of a jiffy, has there been any progress with tracking down the gold? If Amie & Co find out you're getting close, I might need to lay even lower.' Nic nodded. 'Nothing more at this stage. We know the how, almost know the who, and found the where as we've located the plane, so we're off to Alice Springs to check out the what.'

Rose considered her response. 'Well, I've managed to take Hulk out of the picture. John, dressed as you, dressed as Davit Poole managed to throw something up all over him.' Nic responded. 'Throw up what?'

'Julia said it was a mixture of oatmeal, tapioca pudding, and mashed potatoes. It was quite disgusting.' Nic hesitated. 'Do you think Hulk will recognise John and Julia if he sees them again?'

'No, I don't think so as he hasn't met them yet. Besides, John had the "Davit" mask on, and Julia was wearing a full PPE. Why, what are you thinking?'

'I'm thinking it may be best if they get off in Melbourne so they're totally out of the picture.'

Rose nodded. 'OK, I'll have a word with them. Anything else?'

'Yep, we had our first mediation meeting with Elvis and a litany of lawyers representing the woman that was dropped from the helicopter. It went quite well.'

Rose quizzed his comment. 'Why? Didn't the case proceed?

'Oh no, it turned out that Connie, Debacle's wife, has people in high places.'

Rose nodded. 'How high?'

'Her father is a Supreme Court Judge here in Perth, so it's all gone on hold. He's also had a word with the Lead Detective and we've been assigned to investigate both the case of passenger dropsy and the missing gold oopsy.'

Rose nodded again. 'Busy we will be. Anything else?'

Nic continued. 'Only that Detective Kelleigh Brook could be assisting us with the investigation. We're meeting with her later today to see if she'd like to come with us to Alice Springs.'

Rose sighed. 'I'm hanging up now and will call you back later.'

Rose disconnected, then reopened the photograph of Debacle and considered there might just be enough likeness to get away with what she was trying to do, and on the way down to Level 5 her phone chimed. It was a message from Chewy together with the photoshopped picture attached.

The Concierge desk wasn't particularly busy, but Rose had to wait as there were only two staff available. Finally, it was her turn, and she stepped forward. 'I'm wondering if you could help me?'

The attendant smiled. 'Certainly, do you have your cruise pass?'

'Of course.' Rose handed it over and the attendant swiped it through the machine.

'Now, oh...you're in one of The Mansion Suites. I hope you're enjoying your cruise. What seems to be the problem? I'll relocate you to a private office and have one of the other officers sort it out for you. Whatever it is.'

Rose nodded. 'That would be good, thank you. It is quite a delicate matter.'

The attendant picked up the phone and a couple of moments later another attendant walked up to them. 'Please come with me, Ms Jardin. Let's go into the Manager's office. My name is Argyle.'

Rose smiled. 'As in Argyle diamonds?' The man nodded. 'Yes, have you heard of them?' Rose nodded. 'I have a couple of them in my safe at home. I'm always on the lookout for an intense pink one, but they're a little outside my budget.'

The attendant smiled and directed Rose to take a seat. 'Yes indeed, currently worth around five hundred thousand a carat. Now what can I do for you? I don't think we have any Argyle diamonds on board. We did have a beautiful emerald but that sold the other day.'

Rose decided to ignore the comment. 'Do you know who bought it?'

'No, sorry, We're not allowed to disclose the name of the passenger. Safety and all that, anyway, what can I do for you?'

Rose then held up the phone and showed him the photo of herself, Aime, and Debacle in the bar. 'Do you know this man? I believe his name is Nicolai Epine and I can't find him anywhere on board.' The attendant gasped. 'Do you think he's fallen overboard? That means a lot of paperwork.'

Rose shook her head. 'I doubt it, I assume he's sleeping off another heavy drinking session. It's just I.....'

The man nodded. 'I know what you mean. Do you know what cabin he is in?'

'Nope. Are you able to check?'

'I'm not supposed to, but sometimes we have to do what we have to do.'

Rose smiled. 'Don't we know it?'

Argyle tapped at the screen and brought up the list of passengers. 'Nicola Epine you said?... That's odd as there is no record of him boarding the ship. It looks like this photo was taken at the single-ready-to-mingle function on the first night aboard. I'll do a staff listing check.' He pushed a few more buttons. 'Nope, he's not staff either.'

Rose held her breath. 'The other person in the photo said her name was Aime or Amethyst. Does her name come up? Perhaps she knows where he is.'

Argyle ignored Rose's last comment as he was still distracted by the outcome of his searches 'I can't see how he can get on board without being on the manifest. I think we have a major breach of security. If that's the case I'll need to contact the Captain.'

Rose stood up. 'Don't do anything at this stage. I'll do another round of the ship and come back here. He must be on board somewhere, could he be a stowaway?'

Argle sighed heavily. 'No, please...let's not think about that.' Rose shook his hand. 'Thanks anyway. I'll be back.'

Argle put his head into his hands. 'This is an absolute disaster.'

Rose left the office and headed back to her cabin phoning Nic along the way. Yep, you've got me again, Rose. What did Aime say?'

'Nothing yet, I haven't got that far, but there's a slight problem. Chewy didn't add Nicolai's name to the passenger manifest.' Nic called over to Chewy. 'You forgot to add Nicolai to the passenger list.'

'Oops, give me a second while I log into their system. Done.'

Rose called out. 'Thanks, Chewy. I'll call you back when something happens with Aime. Also, I'm about to speak to the J's and tell them to jump ship.'

'OK. Have them take an Uber to Essendon Airport. I'll have a plane ready to fly them back to Sydney, and another car will take them to Epping to collect the Winnebago.' Rose nodded. 'Sounds like a plan. I'll let them know.'

'Sounds like a good plan, Rose. I'll call it...what letter are we up to?'

'It's "H". I'm going now, goodbye.'

Rose disconnected, arrived the J's door and pressed the bell.

Julia called out. 'Who is it?'

'Rosalinda. I'm your neighbour. Can I come in? I've run out of coffee.'

Julia opened the door and Rose quickly moved inside. 'Would you mind leaving the ship? We've decided to let you off here. It's getting all a bit ...um..'

John came out from the bathroom wringing his hands. 'Don't we know it? Julia and I don't know how you do it. It is getting very tense and I think my ulcer has been playing up.' Rose nodded. 'I didn't know you had an ulcer. Did my parents cause that?' John shrugged. 'I think I got it playing golf, it's such a relaxing game. Did you just say we're leaving the ship?'

Rose nodded again. 'Yes, Nic and I think it's the best for all of us.' Julia nodded. 'We were just talking about that. How do we get off without causing a scene?'

Rose shrugged. 'I guess we do it the old-fashioned way and you walk off. I'll write down your itinerary to return to Sydney. Thanks for all this. I'm sorry you only stayed on board for one night.'

Julia began to pack the suitcases, but Rose stopped her. 'It's going to be less conspicuous if you don't take your luggage. I'll sort that out later. Just put it into my cabin, and I'll get it back to you ASAP. You'll only need your cruise cards to disembark. The ship is due to leave here at three, so all you need to do is miss it. They won't wait.'

Twenty minutes later John and Julia disembarked and they were warned that the ship would be leaving at three o'clock and it would not wait for them. John nodded. 'Thank you. We're just having a quick look at CBD and be back in time.'

They left the Cruise Terminal, located their Uber and headed to Essendon Airport as directed. Half an hour later they stepped onto a Lear Jet for the flight to Sydney. They were the only passengers. Julia sat down, buckled herself in, and poured two glasses of champagne. 'I could really get used to this, John.'

Back in Perth, Nic, Chewy and Elvis were in Police HQ for another debrief. The meeting was about to start when Detective Brook's phone rang. 'I'm sorry I have to take this, it's my contact at the Alice Springs Airport.' She moved out of the room to take the call and Nic waited for her to leave. 'I hate it when that happens as we're missing out on the juicy details.' Chewy laughed. 'You do it all the time.'

Nic shrugged. 'I know. I thought I had the monopoly on that move.'

Detective Brook returned so Nic moved to the front of the room to address the small group. 'We have determined that three people were involved in the collection of the bullion. We have recognised them as Amethyst Davey, also known as Aime Davey, and Troy Timpley, aka The Hulk, well, that's what we have been calling him. The third person, who drove the vehicle is unknown at this stage, however, we believe it could be Davida Goldsworthy. They are currently on a cruise ship from Brisbane, heading to Perth, and should arrive in two days where they can be apprehended as required.'

Detective Brook moved to the front of the room. 'We have located the plane that was used to transport the gold. It is in a maintenance hangar at Alice Springs Airport. I'm heading there with Mr Thorn and his associates to secure it for evidence.'

Another Detective referred to her notes and put her hand up. 'Mr Thorn, you mentioned the suspects are on a cruise ship returning to Perth. What is to stop them from disembarking during the journey?'

Nic nodded. 'Good questions. Firstly, I have another one of my associates on the cruise ship who has made her acquaintance with the trio. I am in contact with her daily. Secondly, they are using the, let's say lack of A.M.L compliance of the onboard casino, to convert some of the gold, well let's say cash already held from the conversion of gold, into gambling chips. We are assuming upon arrival they will deposit the accumulated value of the chips into a bank account.'

Detective Brook referred to her notes. 'We have located, who we believe has been assisting the trio trade the gold into cash, and an arrest is imminent. We have not located the pilot of the plane, however, we can now confirm it is Dafydd Barkel, and believe he is in Alice Springs. There is no evidence to suggest otherwise.'

Nic nodded again 'We are aware that Mr Barkel is currently under investigation by CASA regarding a recent incident involving a passenger falling from his helicopter during a flight. We have been told there is a phone-filmed vision of the said incident. We recently met with mediation lawyer, Selwyn

Laab, to view it however the meeting has been rescheduled pending further investigations.'

Detective Brook nodded. 'At this stage, we have not received a copy of the recording. It was anonymously posted to Facebook within hours of the incident and then removed. We have not been able to locate by whom. Our update today confirms I have the approval to join Mr Thorn with the investigation. We leave for Alice Springs on Sunday. Are there any other questions?' Detective Brook looked around the room. 'Good. Meeting closed.' The others exited, leaving Nic, Chewy and Detective Brook in the room. 'What time is the flight on Sunday, Mr Thorn?'

'Please call me, Nic. Mr Thorn is my father.'

'Thanks, Nic. Call me Kelleigh, how about you Mr Chewy?'

'Just call me Chewy, I don't know if wookies have parents. We fly at ten and as it's just under three hours, we should get there for lunch, after the time change.'

Kelleigh nodded 'OK, I'll see you at the airport. I've got some cases to re-allocate and update before I leave.'

Nic and Chewy stood up and left Police HQ to prepare for the trip.

18

Meanwhile, back on the ship, Rose had returned to Level 5. 'Is Argyle available?'

'I'm sorry he's on a break. Can I help?'

'He was checking the passenger manifest for me. I'm trying to locate someone.'

The attendant looked at her. "He's not supposed to do that.' Rose handed over her cruise card again, along with a hundred-dollar note. 'Will this help?'

The attendant nodded. 'Not really, but thanks for the tip. What is the name of the passenger?' Rose nodded. 'Nicolai Epine.'

The attendant grinned. 'Did you know "Epine" is the French word for thorn?'

Rose smiled. 'I did. So, where is he?'

'This says he's in one of the Mansion Suites. Suite 8, next door to you. I'll try the room.' He picked up the phone and Rose could hear the phone ringing through the handset. 'There's no answer. I'll send someone to have a look.'

'Don't worry about that. At least I know where he could be, now I need to find out where he is.' Rose headed back to her cabin and was getting concerned about the "Debacle" photograph so decided to ring her mother to take her mind off things. 'Hello Mother. It's me.' Jana responded quietly. 'What can I do for you, Rosemary? Michael is here, so I can't talk for long. Where are you?'

Rose sighed. 'Still on the cruise. We arrive in Adelaide tomorrow. I hope to catch up with Sandy when I'm there. Her father is still recovering from COVID.' Jana went quiet. 'I'm going now. Rosemary.'

'Hang on, Mother. What's the latest with Father?'

'He's still grumpy, still can't find the diary, still unhappy about my cooking. I have given up trying to please him, so we're eating out a lot these days. Have you heard from Mr and Mrs Croud?'

'I can honestly say, I have no idea where they are at the moment.'

'I'm going now, Rosemary.'

Another voice came through the phone. 'Is that Rose? I want to speak to her.' Jana handed over the phone. 'Hello Rose. It's Michael.'

'What do you want?'

'The diary.'

'How could I have it? I've been on a cruise for the last four days. I'm about to arrive in Adelaide and meet up with Sandy.' Michael went quiet for a moment. 'So, there's no one home at West End?'

'That's none of your business, Michael. Goodbye.'

Rose quickly closed the call and rang Nic. 'Hey, it's me again. I'll make it quick this time. Michael is on the warpath about the diary and it sounds like he's heading to my place to look for it.'

Nic nodded. 'OK. I'll organise a patrol to check it out. Neighbour Dave is looking after Dog doesn't he?'

'Yes, a ten-kilogram cat tends to stay home rather than stray anywhere else. Dave goes in there to feed him and water the plants, that sort of thing.'

'Leave it with me. I'll call you back.'

They disconnected and Rose realised her anxiety levels had risen from the two phone calls rather than lowered, so she decided to change into swimming attire and take a dip in one of the four pools onboard. Rose went to the pool area on Level 9, dropped her towel onto a chair but hadn't noticed Aime and Hulk were next to her.

Aime looked up. 'We're not supposed to be this close, Rosalinda.'

'I'm sorry Aime, I didn't see you there.'

'Not likely. What do you want this time?'

'It's the truth.'

Rose realised it was an opportune moment to show her the photograph of Debacle. 'Do you remember that guy we met in the bar during the single ready to mingle thing? He used my phone to take a selfie of us.' Aime shrugged. 'What of it?'

Rose scrolled to the picture and held up her phone. 'Is this him?' Aime suddenly sat up and the flicker of recognition was obvious. 'That's not him. It's someone else. Again, what of it?'

Rose put the phone down. 'Well, he appears to have gone missing.'

Hulk chortled. 'Did you check the sick bay?'

Rose sighed. 'No, I didn't but the crew on board are about to. They told me he's supposed to be in the cabin next to mine, but I've not seen anyone in there.'

Hulk grunted again. 'There was an old couple in there. They invited me in.'

Rose parked that information. 'Sorry to have bothered you. I'll find another pool.'

Aime nodded and they both stood up. 'Good, you do that. We're taking a dip.'

Rose happened to notice matching "HDT 2015 Fun In Acapulco" tattoos on both of their biceps. 'Nice tattoos by the way. Do they mean anything?'

'Go away, Rosalinda.'

Rose retrieved her towel, decided to take an early lunch, and then called Nic again for any updates. 'Hey, Nic. Me again. Any news?'

Nic chortled. 'Funny you ask. I've just heard Michael is in hospital with a broken arm, suspected broken leg and a myriad of scratches on his face.'

'Oh my God. What happened? Did he disagree with someone?'

'Not someone, something. He thought he could get inside your home via the cat door, and Dog didn't take too kindly to being interrupted from his nap.'

'Dog attacked him?'

'Yep, Michael got his shoulders stuck in the door which left his head exposed on the inside, so Dog thought it was a good idea to teach him a lesson.'

'How did he break his leg?'

'After being battered for about five minutes, Michael finally escaped, fell backwards down the rear stairs and the rest they say is an accident. Attack of the killer cat.'

Rose laughed. 'Good on ya, Dog.'

'Dave, the neighbour heard him crying out and went over the check things out.'

Rose smiled. 'I wouldn't have thought Michael would have been crying out in pain as it would have brought too much attention to his attempted break-in.'

'No, it was Dog that was crying out, but Dave said it could have been laughter.'

'Do you think he'll sue us for having a dangerous animal or anything like that?'

'Not likely. There's no trace of any interaction between Michael and Dog, you know how cats like to keep themselves clean. As far as the police know, he fell down the stairs and landed in a blackberry bush.'

'We don't have a blackberry bush at the bottom of our stairs.'

'Details...details....anyway, anything new on your side?'

'I showed the picture of Debacle to Aime. There was a flicker of recognition, other than that, have you heard of HDT?'

'Holden Dealer Team?'

'No, I don't think so, both Hulk and Aime had matching tattoos that read HDT 2015 Fun In Acapulco.'

'Now that was a great Elvis movie. Ursula Undress at her glowing best, 1963, I believe. Elvis used a stunt double for the hundred-and-thirty-foot high dive.'

'I'm not surprised. The water would feel like concrete from that height. I used to do a little high diving when I trained for surfing. It gets you used to the water hit.'

Rose went quiet for a moment and repeated aloud the tattoo reading. 'HDT Fun in Acapulco. Do you think it could be that they are high divers?'

'Nothing means nothing until it means something doesn't it, Rose?' Rose nodded subconsciously 'I wonder if that's the case. What if the woman that leapt from the helicopter did it deliberately?'

Nic paused. 'Why would she do that?'

'To blackmail a pilot into flying a plane full of gold.'

'You're beginning to think like me.'

Rose sighed. 'Is that a good thing?'

'No, it's scary.'

'Goodbye, Nic. Oh, and do you think I could leave the ship in Adelaide and not get back on? If this thing with Aime and Co. goes pear-shaped, it could get a little uncomfortable being alone with them in the middle of the ocean.'

Nic considered his response. 'It could, apart from the two thousand other people on board, so yep, good idea. Spend some time with Sandy, and catch a commercial flight to Alice Springs when you can. We're heading over there on Saturday and expect to stay about a week.'

'You and Chewy?'

Nic nodded. 'Yep, me and Elvis and Kelleigh.'

'Who is Kelleigh?'

Nic nodded again. 'The Lead Detective on the case.'

'Wow, an upgrade from us...we have a real Detective with us.'

'Yep, at least one of us knows what we are supposed to be doing. See you in Alice, Rose. Oh, one last thing. Chewy just uploaded pictures of the location where Davit discovered the gold nugget. That might make Aime & Co anxious too.'

Rose sighed again. 'Why?'

'Because it's very close to the location we believe they are storing their gold.'

19

It was Sunday morning, and Nic's team were at the Perth Airport waiting for the boarding call. Nic and Kelleigh were seated in Business Class, while Chewy was sitting with Elvis in the three-seat row directly behind them. They had also purchased the middle seat so Chewy could spread his computer and notes. The plane began to taxi, so Chewy shut down the laptop and once airborne he linked into the onboard Wi-Fi to access the web. 'How long have you known him?'

Elvis took a deep breath. 'I met him when we both flew the Erickson Fire helicopters during the New South Wales bushfires in 2001. Lost contact after that, but we reacquainted during that wine scam thing with Nic. He was working freelance then, and picked up that job. After that, we launched the tourist flights to Rottnest Island. Business is good. I guess people can't get enough of those happy quokkas.'

Chewy nodded. 'I didn't get over here then to help bring down that scammer. It was quite an elaborate scam – mislabelling wine bottles and all that stuff.'

Elvis sighed. 'All things must pass I guess.'

Nic had overheard Elvis's comment and decided to raise it with Kelleigh as an ice-breaker. 'Now, that's a great triple album, George at his best. It's even a good seller now.' Kelleigh nodded. 'It's been over twenty years since we lost him, and more than forty since we lost John.'

Nic grinned. 'Beatles fan, Kelleigh?'

'Isn't everyone? I mean there are fans and then there are real fans. I'm closer to the side of the real fans. I've even got a couple of their guitars. One of mine is the Rickenbacker 360/12 like George's, and the other, a Martin D 28 like John's.'

Nic grinned. 'Music to my ears young lady. Do you play them?'

'Every chance I get. I'm in a band with a couple of the D's at HQ. We're called "The Blue Jay Way". Nic nodded. 'Beatles cover band?'

'We cover anyone and everyone. I like to throw in a couple of country songs too, including some from Dusty Springfield and her era.'

'Don't tell Rose, she'll want to join you up on stage.'

'Rose? Is that Rosalinda Jardin?'

'Oh, sorry. It's actually Rose Palmer. We use pseudonyms during our investigations and set up Facebook or LinkedIn sites to verify background info in case someone checks. She's on the cruise with Aime and Co. but will be getting off the boat in Adelaide to catch up with us in Alice.'

'Is she a P.I. too?'

'Not exactly, but she's done the Cert Two. Been working with me for about three years. She's great fun, you'll like her.' Kelleigh nodded. 'Interesting, and I look forward to it. I think I'll get some shut-eye. It's not often I get to fly in the pointy end of the plane. Best enjoy the comfy seat while I can.'

Meanwhile, Chewy had been googling Debacle looking for the alleged CASA infringements. 'Do you know much about the CASA citations? According to this, they're pretty lame.'

Elvis nodded. 'The first one is that Debacle was flying a chopper to a fire emergency and scooped a bucket of water from a domestic swimming pool. The owners didn't like it and wanted to sue. It was a two hundred thousand dollar pool and must have been filled with Evian.' Chewy grinned. 'And the second?'

'He was flying a fixed-wing, Boeing 737 Fireliner, and got too close when he dropped the fire retardant, and it turned the roof of a house pink.'

'And he could lose his licence for that?'

'Probably not, but it's better not to have any citations, rather than a couple of them lodged by disgruntled homeowners. It's disappointing to have it hanging over our heads.' Chewy continued searching. 'OK. What about his personal life, do you think he's involved in this gold scam?'

'Nope, well at least I hope not. He's as straight-laced as they come. Loves his kids and Connie, and often reminds me how lucky he is to live and work in the great state of W.A.'

'Anything else you can think of? What about hobbies?'

'He's a mad West Coast Eagles fan. He told me once he hasn't missed a home game since they last won the grand final in 2018 against Collingwood. Just likes to keep the hope going. They haven't been playing well of late.'

Chewy nodded. 'No other hobbies?'

'Not really. Oh, I forgot. He is a face painter too.'

'Painting kid's faces, like at parties and things? Does he dress up like a clown?'

Elvis laughed. 'No, for football games. He paints one side of his face yellow and the other royal blue. The Eagles colours. He's got one of their premium membership packages too, which provides the members with discounted hotel accommodation, that sort of thing.'

Chewy grinned. 'I'm a Hawthorn fan myself, but no one wants to have brown and yellow paint smeared over your face. It's not a good look. I think there's a game in Alice Springs on Monday. The Hawks are playing The Eagles.'

Elvis smiled. 'Looks like we'll be going to a footy game then.' Chewy nodded. 'Well, that might make things a little bit easier for us.' Elvis shrugged. 'They play at Traeger Park. On a good day, it holds about ten thousand people, but against the Hawks, who knows? Probably a little less.'

Chewy stood up to see if Nic was awake. He wasn't, so he sat back down. 'Those seats must be very comfortable. They're both asleep.'

Around two hours later the plane was taxiing along the tarmac and they were permitted to turn their phones back on. Nic opened his phone and there was a message from Rose: '*The photo has got them spooked. Hulk has been running around like Dorothy the Dinosaur at a Wiggles concert. I'm definitely getting off in Adelaide. We arrive at two. It's getting a bit ugly. Oh, and ring me when you've got settled. I've thought of something else.*'

The foursome arrived in Alice Springs and collected a pair of Land Cruisers from the airport car hire. Chewy drove one with Elvis and Nic asked Kelleigh to drive the other. They had also utilised Debacle's Eagles membership to secure the last two rooms available at the Hilton Double Tree on Barrett Drive. Nic, Elvis and Chewy would be sharing a triple while Rose would have a twin with Kelleigh.

Nic unloaded his luggage and went to the outside bar to return the call to Rose. 'Hey, Rose. We've arrived. What's up?'

Rose whispered. 'They're now putting up posters "Have you seen this man?" And it was just announced by the Captain they might have lost a person overboard.'

'OK, we might have to deal with that later. There are still two sea days before arriving in Perth. He'll turn up somewhere.'

'That's not what I'm concerned about. It's what happens when the cruise ship arrives in Perth and neither you nor I are on it?'

'That one you'll definitely have to leave with me. I might still go with Plan A.'

Rose sighed. 'I thought Plan A was that you were to stay in my cabin until you could relocate to the wedding suite.'

Nic nodded. 'Oh, I thought Plan A was that you and I were to be in jail so Aime and Co. wouldn't come looking for us to get their money back.'

Rose shook her head. 'Nope. That one didn't get a letter. So, how can you make that happen?'

'Leave that one with me too.'

Nic closed the call and the others ambled up. 'Lunch anyone?'

Elvis nodded. 'And drinks are on me, well Debacle anyway, as his membership gives us a discount at the bar too.'

Nic shook his head. 'I think it's best if we stick to zero alcohol as we don't want to draw attention to ourselves.'

Kelleigh nodded. 'Good idea. So, what's to plan for the rest of the day?'

Nic smiled and held up his phone showing the Facebook post he had been talking to Rose about. 'We're taking a drive out to where Davit Poole found the gold.'

Elvis leaned in. 'What gold and who is Davit Poole?'

Chewy smiled. 'He's Rosalinda Jardin's ex-husband's lawyer, who recently found a gold nugget out this way near where Aime and Co. have stored their stolen gold.'

Elvis sat back. 'When did Rose get married?'

Nic grinned. 'No question about the gold? You just want to know if Rose is off the market?'

Elvis shrugged.

Kelleigh had been fully debriefed on the scale of Nic's team's investigation, so decided to add a comment. 'Davit is still on the cruise with Rose, along with Nicolai Epine, however both appear to have gone AWOL. We hope to be arresting one or both of them in Perth.'

Elvis shook his head. 'Nic said Rose is not going to Perth, she's meeting us here later this week.'

Chewy opened his laptop, made a few keystrokes, and spun it around so Elvis could look at the picture. It was the one of him standing with Davit Poole holding the gold nugget. 'That's me...but I didn't pose for this.'

Chewy continued. 'Meet Davit Poole, gold prospector and not-so-nice-guy lawyer.'

Elvis looked a little closer. 'They look like your skinny legs, Chewy.'

Nic nodded. 'Yep, it's a cut and paste. It's amazing what you can do with pictures from Facebook if you have the technology.'

Kelleigh held up her phone. 'I've got Magic Photo Editor on this one too. It's great for removing those pesky little things that get in your way when you take pictures of evidence at a crime scene.' They all looked at her. 'Only joking.'

The group laughed and Nic continued. 'It's about a two-hour drive south to Erlunda Roadhouse. Then we take a right onto The Lassiter Highway and head west for another bit, then take another right and head north for another bit, toward Petermann.' Chewy nodded. 'And somewhere out there we'll find Lassiter's Reef, although we might rename it "Aime and Co's Gold Hide-e-Hole."'

Nic nodded again. 'So, let's regroup in about an hour. We'll leave here at two and should be back around nine tonight depending on how many times we have to stop for kangaroos and emus.'

Elvis shook his head. 'You shouldn't drive after dusk in the NT. The wildlife don't follow the road rules and tend to freeze in the glare of bright headlights.'

'Yep, so can everyone pack a light kit as tonight we're staying in a six-berth cabin at the Ayers Rock Campground. We'll have a 6:30 start in the morning, then head north, have a bit of look for the gold and be back here by tomorrow arvo for a footy game.'

20

An hour later the group re-grouped and headed south in one of the Cruisers. Elvis was driving, Kelleigh riding shotgun with Nic and Chewy in the rear seats. 'It's four and a half hours to Uluru so we'll be there before dark. Keep it under the limit, Elvis.'

'We're on the Stuart, so I can go one-thirty.'

'Yep, but we don't want to be stopped by the Police and explain what we're doing out here do we?' Kelleigh smiled. 'I've never had to talk my way out of a ticket, but then I've never been involved in a hunt for gold either. First time for everything.' Elvis responded. 'OK. Next question. How do you know the gold is out this way? It could be anywhere.'

Chewy opened a folio on the seat and began to read from his notes. 'To date, Aime and Co. have applied for eighty -six mining permits, including the NT, WA and South Australia. The Task Force has been monitoring their emails and phone intercepts for the last six months and in March the activity began to escalate. Then we saw the use of words like Giggle, Gumby and Gilt began to increase, so they ran an AI programme through it to identify any locations. We've only got to the area, not the actual site.'

Kelleigh smiled. 'I'm not going to ask about how you manage to monitor a closed system, or how you know such a Government-operated programme even exists.'

Chewy shrugged and Elvis nodded. 'So, it's been planned for quite some time. Why not just arrest them?'

Kelleigh sighed. 'They hadn't done anything. You don't need to get a licence to go fossicking and we, well lost interest in them.'

Nic nodded. 'There's so much stuff like this going on around the place, that's why there's room for people like me to monitor stuff for people like them. Otherwise, the whole system would be stuffed as it's bogged down in stuff.'

The team made good time and arrived at The Erlunda Roadhouse in just under two hours. Elvis shut down the engine, climbed out, and stretched. 'I think I'll get another case of water bottles, anyone want anything?'

Kelleigh nodded. 'I'll come too. Give you a hand.'

Chewy stepped out and left the doors open to allow fresh air inside. 'Another two hours to go. I guess we'll be able to enjoy the Uluru sunset on the rock. I can tick that one off my bucket list.' Nic stepped out and joined him. 'I'm not sure yet.'

'Why?'

'Because I've been thinking about Debacle and how he fits into all of this. Rose mentioned that he could just be an innocent bystander, and they could have blackmailed him into flying the plane. It sort of makes sense.'

Chewy nodded 'So, how does that explain why he has gone to ground?'

'Maybe he hasn't, it's just we can't find him but we haven't really looked.' Nic took a breath and continued. 'If it is the case that Aime or Davida jumped from the helicopter as they knew of his two other CASA citations, it wouldn't be much of a leap to influence him to become involved.'

Chewy nodded. 'So, let's just say the chip does show something happening on the flight, it would be his priority to keep it safe. I think we're looking in the wrong place. Finding him should be our priority, not the gold.'

Elvis and Kelleigh returned, each juggling a six-pack of water. Elvis loaded the water into the boot and handed a bottle to each of the others. 'It was on special and you can never be without enough water. Next stop, The Rock.'

Nic took a long drink. 'Actually, we're going back to Alice Springs.'

Elvis looked at him. 'We're doing what now?'

'Getting back into the car.' Nic was about to elaborate. 'Hold that thought.' He then moved over to an old Volkswagen Combi that a family group of six had just piled out from. They looked like they hadn't seen the inside of a hotel room for months. Four headed inside while the driver and a young boy remained by their car. Nic seized them up. 'Where are you guys heading?'

The boy looked up at him. 'Dad told me that we're heading to see the rock. He's my favourite movie star. I loved him as the Tooth Fairy.' The boy grinned to reveal a mouthful of missing teeth. 'I'm waiting for this one to drop.'

The father wandered closer. 'Can I help you, mate?'

'Your boy said you're heading to the rock. Do you have a booking at the campsite yet?'

The man nodded back at the van. 'Nope. Living in the bug. Free campers.'

'Well, my guys are booked there tonight but we're heading back to Alice instead. Would you like to use the cabin?'

Meantime, his partner had returned from purchasing supplies and looked at him. 'What's going on?'

Nic held up his hands defensively. 'Nothing. It's just that it's too late to cancel the booking and it will go empty. I can see if it can be extended if you want to stay longer.'

The little boy looked up to Nic. 'Are you Santa?'

'Not quite, but it's yours if you want it, and as the entry works on a PIN entry system, It will be OK. I'll put it into your phone if you allow me.'

The man handed over this phone, looked around at his horde, and clapped his hands. 'Climb back in kids. We're going to see the rock and stay in a place with running water, a flushing toilet, and Bluey on a TV.' The children were cheering and singing as they drove off.

Nic moved back to his group and climbed into the car. 'Now, let's get back to Alice and start hunting Debacle.'

Kelleigh shrugged. 'Nice thing you did there. I've often wanted to pay things forward but being a cop, people treat you very suspiciously.'

Elvis turned the Cruiser around and they headed east, towards Alice Springs. 'As I said before, we're doing what now?'

Nic called out. 'We're hunting a Debacle. We know where he isn't, so we have about two hours before it gets dark, to work out where he could be.'

Elvis called back. 'Where isn't he?'

Kelleigh responded. 'At the Hilton Double Tree on Barrett Drive. I guess we start from there and work outwards.'

Chewy nodded. 'If all that fails, we will have to wait until the footy game tomorrow.'

21

They arrived back in Alice Springs around five o'clock. Elvis and Chewy went to the bar while Nic decided to call Rose but couldn't reach her, and Kelleigh went to her room to call her people. They agreed to meet back for dinner at seven.

Chewy opened his laptop and started looking at other places of accommodation and sites that Debacle may have visited, stayed, or anything that may bring them closer to finding him. 'There's more than a hundred places to stay if you include backpackers and Airbnb's. Any ideas about how we can reduce the search?'

Elvis nodded. 'Does anything else have accommodation arrangements with The Eagle members?' Chewy shook his head. 'Not really. The offer is for premium package members only, so the general members are on their own.'

Elvis sighed. 'What about anything to do with pilots or aircraft or aviation? He might get a discount through the Australian Pilots Association.'

Chewy shook his head again. 'Nothing there either, and the commercial plane staff stay here too.' Elvis sat back and clasped his fingers together. 'Can you check to see if the Central Australian Aviators Museum has accommodation? It's not near the airport but it might be somewhere he could have visited.'

Chewy was tapping away when Nic and Kelleigh returned. Nic held out a chair for Kelleigh and then took a seat himself. 'Find anything?'

Elvis nodded. 'I've been thinking about what you said, "We know where he isn't, so we have to work out where he could be."'

Nic smiled. 'Yep, that was one of my better ones.'

Elvis continued. 'Well, let's assume that he flew the plane under duress and doesn't know anybody here. On that basis, I think he'll look for familiarity. Somewhere safe to hide.'

Nic opened his phone and located the Aviator museum's website. 'They open at nine. So we'll start there.'

They were finishing the meals and Chewy noticed a band was setting up on the stage. 'Looks like live music is on tonight and the sign says anyone can join in. Are you up for it Nic?' Kelleigh grinned. 'You didn't mention that you play too.'

Nic nodded. 'I've currently got five guitars, including a 1972 Hoffner Viola bass. I keep that one under glass in my warehouse in Brisbane along with a couple of my early Beatle album presses, including a mint condition "Butcher Album."'

Kelleigh smiled. 'So definitely a Beatles fan.'

Nic shrugged. 'I would say a healthy obsession. Would you be up to playing a couple of songs? We might be able to flush out Debacle even if he's not staying here. It looks like quite a few Eagles members have started to arrive.'

Kelleigh nodded 'So, what are you thinking?'

'Let's do "Call Me the Breeze" by JJ Cale. It's twelve-bar in E, then ramp up the next one. It's in the same key.'

'What's the next one?'

'The West Coast Eagles Football Club song.'

Kelleigh smiled 'That should work. I'll set it up,' and she headed off to have a word with the emcee.' Nic took a long drink of his Heineken Zero. 'So, while we're up there doing our thing can you two guys walk the floor and see if anyone knows him or has seen him around.' Chewy nodded. 'Sounds like a plan. The show winds up at eleven so it gives us about four hours of wandering.'

Kelleigh returned. 'We're the second act up. I told them what songs we were doing and they reckoned it would get the crowd going for the main act. They wanted me to sign a liability waiver for using their equipment but I refused.'

Nic nodded. 'Yet, they're still letting us play?'

'I flashed them my badge and that calmed them down a bit. You don't do any high-kicks or anything do you?' Nic shook his head. 'Only when I play KISS songs. Do you want me to run through the Eagles song with you?'

'No, I've played that before too, but I prefer the original. They changed the club song a couple of years ago, so I have learned both just in case.'

The first group finished so Nic and Kelleigh moved to the stage area, while Chewy and Elvis began their search for Debacle. It didn't take long for the crowd to be in rapture and the Eagles Club song finally wound down. The duo thanked the band for the use of the guitars and sat back down. Chewy had returned but Elvis wasn't around. 'Any luck?'

'Nothing, most of the crowd were doing the singing thing with you guys. I got nowhere, but come to think of it I was using a portrait of Debacle without his blue and gold face paint.'

Kelleigh grinned. 'Where's Elvis?'

'I don't know. He said something about his phone, so I assume he's taken it to his room.'

Nic went quiet. 'Was he carrying it when you were doing your search?'

Chewy shook his head. 'I assume so. He went one way and I went the other. We met back here, then he took off again.'

Nic rang Elvis and he didn't answer. 'OK, that's not good.' He then tapped on his "Locate-My-Friend" app and it showed the phone was not turned on.

They quickly moved over to the bar and asked the staff whether they'd seen him.

The barman shook his head. 'Nope, but someone found a phone in the men's toilet. It's not one of ours. Is this his?' He reached down below the bar, collected the phone, and held it out to them.

Nic nodded. 'Yep, it's his.'

Kelleigh reached inside her pocket and showed the barman her badge. 'Do you have CCTV?'

'Yeah, but....' Nic leaned forward. 'But what?'

'It only points at the cash registers and the fridges. We're not allowed to take any vision of people dancing or anything. Too many complaints.'

Nis took a step back. 'Damn it, Elvis. Where are you?'

Kelleigh looked around. 'Let's try your room.'

The trio hustled to the room and Nic carefully opened the door. Elvis wasn't there. 'Come on, Elvis, Don't do this to me.'

Nic sighed. 'OK, it's too late now to do anything more tonight. Let's sleep on it and start again in the morning.'

Nic and Chewy were waiting for Kelleigh at breakfast. Elvis was still missing, and Nic hadn't been able to contact Rose. That too was concerning him. He was about to try again when his phone rang. It was Driver from Adelaide. They had used Driver as a driver to drive them around Adelaide when they investigated an invoice scam a few years ago. 'Hey, Driver. What's up?'

'Have you talked to Rose yet?'

'Isn't she still in Adelaide?'

'Nope. When I collected Rose I expected her to want to catch up with Sandy and her Father, but we had to change plans. We were sitting in the car and she was updating me on the gold thing when she noticed Aime and Co. coming off the ship?' Nic nodded. 'They could've been spending a day in Adelaide.'

'That's what we thought too until they collected their luggage and jumped into a cab. So, we followed them to the airport.'

'Do you know where they went?'

'They chartered a private plane to Alice Springs. Rose also took a plane out of Adelaide last night. They left an hour earlier and would have arrived late afternoon yesterday. The flight time is about two hours, but you gain an hour as the NT doesn't do daylight savings.'

'What makes you think they flew to Alice Springs?'

'I managed to find that out from Airport Security. I told them I was their chauffeur and had been diagnosed with COVID again, and I needed to let my passengers know. They called through to the pilot.'

Nic nodded. 'That changes a few things here. Do you know why Rose is not answering her phone?'

'Nope. Let me know if you need me to join you up there.'

'Will do, and thanks for the update, mate. Take care of yourself.'

'Will do, Boss...oops sorry, Nic.'

Nic disconnected and looked at Chewy. 'Did you get most of that?'

Chewy nodded. 'So, they're here and Elvis is missing. Is there a connection?'

'I hope not. What about Rose?'

Nic opened up his phone and rang Rose. They could hear a phone ringing. It was getting closer. Nic looked up and smiled. 'Morning Rose, glad to see you turned your phone from flight mode. Would you like to join us for breakfast?'

Kelleigh arrived a few moments later. 'You're right, Nic. I like her.' Rose shrugged. 'Sorry about that, Nic. I decided to go straight to the room and freshen up before calling you. I fell asleep. Kelleigh has updated me about Elvis and the gold. So, what's the what now?'

Nic continued. 'Well, you're here and you're safe. This morning we're heading to the Aviators Museum to check that out. Elvis thought that might be a place to start. Even if Debacle is not there he may have been there, and if that comes to nothing we'll drive around and check out other hotels and stuff. Then we'll go to the football game. It starts at one.'

Chewy nodded. I've got an idea about using the local television coverage to try to find him if he is at the footy. Has anyone heard of Kiss-Cam?'

Nic grinned. 'That might just work, but it sometimes gets embarrassing when they show people on the giant television screen that don't want to be involved.'

Rose sighed. 'Or they're sitting by themselves. I had that done to me once.' Kelleigh nodded. 'Or they're there and not supposed to be with the one they're with. I've seen that one too, at a Coldplay Concert.' Nic grinned. 'As they say, if you can't love the one you want, love the one you're with. Stephen Stills wrote that classic.'

Chewy continued. 'So let's finish breakfast and meet back here in twenty minutes.' The group nodded and headed back to their rooms.

22

Elvis opened his eyes but there was nothing but blackness, so he raised his hands only to realise they were bound together, then he tried to stretch them apart and felt the pull of a plastic cord between his wrists. He muttered aloud: 'They're tied together.'

Elvis knew he was in a sitting position, so softly lowered his hands to the floor. It felt cold to the touch and metallic. 'Where the hell am I?'

A voice responded from the darkness. 'You're in an old aeroplane fuselage. Both ends are sealed. That's why it's so dark in here.'

'Is that you, Debacle?'

'Yeah, it looks like we're in this together now.'

'They found you then. We've been looking for you too. Where are we?'

'At the Aviator Museum. I've been hiding here for a week. I think they've been on a cruise or something. I heard them talking about it.'

'Three of them?'

'Yeah, they mentioned another couple of other names too. Rosalinda something, a Nicolai Epine and some old dude, Davit Poole. Apparently, he's found a gold nugget, but they reckon it's all a bit sus.'

'"Rosalinda" is Rose Palmer and works with Nic. I've been helping him out and we've got a Detective from Perth with us too. We've been looking for the gold, and you.'

Debacle sighed. 'Who are the other two guys?'

Elvis's eyes had become accustomed to the lack of light and he could see Debacle's silhouette directly opposite him. His hands were also tied. He wasn't wearing the Eagles cap. 'They're both Nic. He uses disguises and stuff like that. They've been following Aime and Co. Are they here now?'

'They were here, but they've taken the van and are loading the gold onto it. Something has got them spooked. If I lose them now, they'll be able to hide the gold forever.'

Elvis went quiet for a moment. 'So, why did you fly the planc?'

Debacle lowered his head. 'They know about Connie and the girls. Threatened to ...you know. I've got to get my cap back. It's in the back of the van along with my phone.' Elvis grinned. 'I promise to buy you another one.'

'No, it's the cap. It's got the chip in it. I wrapped it in tissue paper and put it on the inside of the visor. They have my phone too, in the van. I'm so stupid.'

'You're not mate, sometimes things happen. It's what you do afterwards that makes all the difference. Tell me about the passenger that fell out of the plane.'

Debacle looked up. 'It was that woman, Aime. She jumped. She didn't fall. It's all on the chip, the vision. She knew about the CASA third strike policy, I just made a stupid decision to allow myself to....' Debacle stopped talking and looked down again. Elvis sighed. 'Mate, it will get sorted. Are you hurt?'

'No, it's just ...I'm so sorry Elvis.'

'Mate, we'll sort it out. How did they find you here?'

'They used that app. I turned my phone on. I wanted to call Connie. It was only on for about ten minutes. I rang her, but she didn't answer. I didn't leave a message. I didn't know what to say. They turned up Sunday arvo and found me.

'Is the phone still on?'

'I assume so. Why?'

'Because that means Nic will be able to track it down. He might not be able to find us, but at least he'll find them.' Elvis managed to stand up and made his way over to Debacle and draped his arms over his shoulders. 'Bring it in, mate. Just don't tell anyone that two guys are having a hug.'

Nic and his crew drove to the museum and stood outside the locked gates wondering why the site wasn't open for business. Rose took a sniff of the air. 'Can you smell that?' Nic looked at her. 'I can. What is it? It's not avgas. There's something else. It smells like something burnt.'

Kelleigh took a walk along the perimeter fence. 'Smells like a fire. I can call it in, and maybe we can get access.' Kelleigh opened her phone and called the local Fire Brigade, identified herself as a Detective, nodded a few times, and then closed the call. 'There was a fire here last night. Nothing major. It's just they're not going to be opening for a couple of days until things are cleaned up. Started in a wheely-bin at the back of the office.'

Nic smiled. 'No witnesses, no cameras, that sort of thing?'

'Yeah, something like that. No real damage.'

Rose nodded. 'Just enough damage to keep any prying eyes out of the place.'

Kelleigh smiled. 'You're very suspicious, aren't you? Who would do that?' Rose continued, 'Nic has told us that nothing means nothing until it means something. So, in this case, here is a place with access to aeroplane equipment and plenty of storage, and we can't get in to look because of a recent fire.'

Nic smiled. 'Please go on, Rose.'

'Well, it's the first place we want to search for our elusive missing pilot and we can't get access. I wonder if we'll find the same thing at any other places.'

Chewy nodded. 'Well, only one way to find out. Let's head off and start with the local shops. He must've been buying food and drinks somewhere if he was here.'

They climbed back into the Cruiser and tried a few of the local shops. No one had seen a man of Debacle's description loitering around. It didn't help that the only photograph they had didn't have him wearing the Eagles cap. They split up and tried a few hotels around the central business district, then met up again at the Alice Springs Information Centre. Nic sighed. 'Debacle is a real Nowhere Man. That was one of The Beatles best songs.'

As it was now getting closer to game time, they decided to head off early to Traeger Park. Nic paid the admission fee for the four of them and Chewy headed off to find the television broadcasting unit. Kelleigh went with him. Nic took a moment with Rose. 'This is one of the ugliest ones we've been involved in so far, isn't it?' Rose nodded. 'I guess money talks and people listen, in this case, it's a golden goose. But we'll catch them, it's what we do.'

Nic smiled. 'Technically, it's not a scam or a fraud, it's straight-out theft.'

Chewy returned. 'All set up. They will announce at the start of the game they're trialling "Kiss-Cam" and hopefully he will turn up if he's here. They've given me remote access to a camera so I can scan the crowd.' Nic nodded. 'Rose and I will wander around the ground to see if anyone has seen him. Where's Kelleigh?'

'She stayed with the OB van to watch things from in there.'

Nic and Rose headed over to the grandstand and took a seat. They were looking for the camera when the announcement came over the loudspeakers. *"Game On. Welcome to fans of the Hawks and Eagles. We have a great day planned and fun for everyone. Please be aware we are trailing Kiss-Cam today, so if you see your beautiful faces up on the large screen, don't be shy and give it a try. And here's our first couple...hopefully they are a couple...if not they might have some explaining to do..."*

Rose looked up and the screen and recognised her face, then the vision expanded to include Nic. 'It's us. What do you want to do?' Nic smiled. 'Kiss me.' Rose sighed, puckered up, kissed the back of her hand and then wiped it on Nic's cheek. The crowd cheered, then the screen went blank. Nic grinned. 'I don't think it supposed to happen like that. Never mind.'

The game started with a flurry of goals by The Hawks and by three-quarter time The Eagles were in front by a single point. Chewy had been scanning the crowd, however, as most of the Eagles supporters either had their faces painted or were being obstructed by flags and banners it was difficult to focus on any one person. Eventually, he gave up and just looked for couples that were happy to kiss. The game finished in a draw, and the crowd slowly shuffled away. The trio met in the grandstand again, and Chewy was shaking his head. 'Didn't work. Too many face painters and too many people wearing caps and hats. At least it was a good game.'

Nic stood up, helped Rose to rise and they were heading toward the car when his phone rang. It was Connie. 'Hey, Nic. Have you found him?'

'Nup, not yet.' Connie continued. 'Oh, it's just that I saw you on the television. You were at the footy game. The Kiss-cam thing. You were looking relaxed. Who was the woman that gave you the cold shoulder? It was very funny, even my girls laughed. I haven't heard them do that since he left.'

'That was Rose. She was on the cruise with Aime and Co. but has joined us here in Alice to help find him. What makes you think we found him?'

'He rang me. I missed the call. He must have turned his phone on. It's got that "Find My Phone" app on it. It's showing that he's in Alice Springs. I thought he was with you.'

Nic hesitated. 'Does it show where is?'

'He was heading west along the B6 but appears to have stopped in Larapinta. It's a small suburb just out of town.'

Nic held out his phone. We've found him. Heading west towards the MacDonnell Ranges. Let's get to the car. We'd better move as there's a chance we'll lose network if he gets out much further.' The others quickly moved to the Cruiser and Nic closed the call. 'I promise I'll get him to call you back when I find him, Connie.'

23

Both Elvis and Debacle had managed to sever the ties on a shard of metal and were in the process of kicking through the closed ends of the plane, however, as it was still dark, they couldn't see if they were having any success. Elvis took a breath. 'Any other ideas, mate?'

'I've got one, but you may not like it.'

'Hit me.'

'We're inside the shell of a 737, and I recall this one still has a door attached. If we can find it, we can blow the bloody doors off and release the emergency shute.'

'Why is that a problem?'

'If it's faulty, or old. It may blow us up instead.'

Elvis nodded. 'Find it, do it, blow it and let's get the hell out of here.'

'Found it.'

'That was quick.'

'I was standing next to it, I just didn't know if you would go for it.'

Elvis made his way over to the door and together they managed to get it open then sunlight flooded into the space. Elvis looked down. 'It's too far to jump. We have to use the shute.' Debacle nodded, flicked the top panel and was about to pull down the shute lever but hesitated. 'On three.'

Elvis also put his hand on the lever. 'Three.'

The gas blew, the shute opened and then unfurled onto the ground. They jumped on and slid down. 'Where to now?' Debacle began to run. 'The office. There's a desk phone in there. I'm going to call Connie.'

Elvis nodded. 'Do that, keep it quick, then I'll call Nic.'

They arrived outside the office and used the fire-damaged wheely bin as a makeshift ladder to scramble through a broken window. The phone was working, and Debacle called Connie. 'It's me, Connie. I'm safe. Still in Alice.'

'Thank God, you scared us. What have you got yourself into?'

'I can't say much now. I'll explain it all when I get home later this week.'

'Is Nic with you?'

'Just Elvis. Why?'

'Oh, he must be chasing down the gold. I told him they're heading west on Highway 6.'

'How do you know that?'

'Find My Phone app. That's how I knew to tell Nic you were still in Alice.'

'Of course. Wow, that gives me an idea. I've got to go now, Connie. Give my love to the girls and see you soon.' He hung up and Elvis called Nic but it was a poor connection. 'I'll be quick, Nic. We're at the museum. Aime and Co. are heading west on Highway 6.'

The response from Nic was sketchy. 'Don't...look...for...' The call terminated and Elvis held out the phone. 'They must be out of range.'

Debacle looked at him, then at the ground, then at the ex-Army Chinook Helicopter parked on the museum paddock, then back at Elvis. 'How long has it been since you flew one of those?'

Elvis shook his head. 'Not since we worked together fighting the fires in New South Wales in' 01. Why, what are you thinking?'

'They keep it here as part of their exhibition and I know it runs as they have to keep it on standby. Would you like to come gold prospecting with me? I've heard they're a large gold deposit on Highway 6, somewhere west of Alice Springs.'

Elvis grinned. 'But how does that help us stop them? If we land, they'll drive around us, so all we can do is hover over them, but they can keep driving. We'll run out of fuel before they will.' Debacle shrugged, climbed in, put the headphones on and began the pre-flight checks.

The twin rotors began to turn and they were soon airborne. A call came through their headphones: *"This is Alice Springs Airport. Please state your name and your heading. You do not have approval in this airspace."*

Elvis took the response. 'My name is Aron Preslin. My co-pilot is Dafydd Barkel. We are in pursuit of a stolen shipment of gold along Highway 6. Please contact Detective Kelleigh Brook for any further details.' Elvis then switched off the radio. 'We don't need any distractions at the moment. We've got some gold to catch.'

Somewhere underneath them, Rose and Nic were in the back seat of the Cruiser and Kelleigh was riding shotgun. Chewy was struggling to get the large car up to a hundred and thirty. 'They won't be able to go above eighty. The gold would be too heavy, and they'd need to conserve fuel.'

Nic called out. 'Yep, but keep under the speed limit anyway.'

Rose was reading the Road Atlas. 'Did you say they were heading west? There's nothing out there.' Nic nodded. 'Yep, nothing but places to hide gold bullion. It won't rust, won't tarnish and be around longer than we will ever be. A legacy for their kids and grandkids to enjoy in perpetuity.'

Kelleigh smiled. 'So, it's true, there is gold out this way. Lassiter was right.'

Chewy managed to avoid a large dead kangaroo. 'Roadkill. Dangerous at any time of day. I hope we can catch up to them soon, but I don't know what will happen when we do.' Nic nodded again. 'We'll think of some....' He had to stop mid-sentence due to the loud noise of a helicopter flying overhead. 'They're flying very low.'

Debacle drew the yoke towards himself to gain height. 'We're too low, I'm going higher. Easier to spot them.' They had flown about another hundred kilometres west when Elvis pointed to a white van in the distance. 'They've stopped. It looks like they might have hit something.' Debacle lowered the speed of the helicopter. 'Not stopped, just going slowly. That's a whole lot of gold to carry in a small HiAce van like that one.'

Elvis responded. 'It's reinforced. They strengthened the chassis and added the roof rack. That's what they did to the one left behind in Perth, I assume it's been modified to the same specs.'

Debacle grinned. 'That gives me an idea. Can you fly solo for a while? I've got an appointment with a winch.'

Elvis took control and heard movement behind him, then he felt the rush of incoming air. It was then he what Debacle was going to do. 'Are you going fishing?'

Debacle nodded. 'Something like that, but I'm not the bait, just the weight.'

Elvis turned around, saw that Debacle had fastened the winch hook around his waist and he stepped out into the space. The next thing he saw was Debacle dangling from a wire and called out to him. 'So it's Mission Possible, Mr Hunt.'

Elvis steadied the helicopter while Debacle used the winch control to lower himself to the van. It didn't take long and he was hovering over it.

Debacle softly stepped onto the roof, undid the winch hook, threaded through the roof rack and cross-tied it through the sides. He gave Elvis a thumbs up, and began to ascend on a second winch wire.

Debacle stepped back into the helicopter and took a bow. 'I saw it on TV.' Elvis slowly pulled on the yoke, they gained a little height and the wire went taught. 'I hope they've got their seatbelts on.'

About a kilometre away, Chewy took his foot from the accelerator as the helicopter was now flying towards them. He stopped the Cruiser and they all climbed out. Nic pointed towards the noise, and at the HiAce van dangling from the wire. 'It looks like someone has been fishing.'

24

Nic's team drove back to Alice Springs and they headed to the museum where Elvis and Debacle were waiting with their catch of the day. Kelleigh had already rung ahead to make sure Aime and Co were detained pending the arrest. The local Police were waiting when they arrived. Kelleigh debriefed them on the situation and the arresting Sergeant looked over to the Chinook. 'So you're telling me that someone just flew this old bucket of bolts to go fishing, and hooked up a great white HiAce van full of gold?'

Elvis nodded. 'Something like that, but the truth of the matter is that my friend wanted to retrieve his West Coast Eagles cap. It was his favourite one.'

Kelleigh assisted Aime and Co. to step out of the front of the van and Debacle opened the rear doors. He leaned in. located his cap and put it on. 'Yeah, that's about it. It's my only one too.'

They placed the trio into a Paddy Wagon, and the police drove them away to be processed.

Nic stepped into the back of the van and did a rough count of the ingots. 'I reckon around two hundred and sixty. It's no wonder they were going slow as that would weigh over two thousand kilos.' Kelleigh decided to join him and noticed a black barrel bag. 'Some of the cash?' She opened the bag and it contained around thirty thousand in cash, and a handful of casino chips from the cruise ship. 'We must have really spooked them as they didn't have time to convert these to something they could actually use.'

Nic nodded. 'And I've got another twenty grand stored in a bank deposit box in Newcastle.'

Kelleigh grinned, reached into the bag and extracted the emerald. 'I assume this is yours?'

Nic smiled. 'You can keep it as a memento of our time together.'

Kelleigh sighed. 'What about the gold nugget, is that a fake too?'

Nic grinned. 'Chewy did a good mock-up of that. It was a cut and paste.'

Kelleigh continued. 'And what about the Tiffany necklace Rose was wearing last night? Is that a fake too?' Nic smiled. 'Oh, no that is real. No one can fake Tiffany.'

The group then watched as the contents of the van was secured and driven off to the police holding area. Nic approached Elvis. 'That was very risky and not at all what I was planning to do.' Elvis shrugged. 'I wasn't planning to do that either. I didn't have a plan.'

Kelleigh was about to add her comment when her phone rang, so she moved away to take the call and returned a few moments later. 'They found the rest of the gold in a storage facility at Jandakot Airport. Tallied up to be one-forty ingots in total. The guy was just handing over the cash and admitted it that much gold was too big for him to handle. He hadn't got around to working out how he was going to melt it all down, let alone find someone interested in it. He was just a small-time jeweller.'

Rose smiled. 'So, was any of the gold melted down?'

Kelleigh shook her head. 'As far as we know, none of it. It's going to be an interesting trial if it ever gets to that. At this point, all they are guilty of is handing over a stolen Bank Cheque, and that part will be up to the Bank to pursue.'

Debacle sighed. 'She did threaten to hurt Connie and my kids, and forced me to fly to Alice Springs.' Kelleigh again shook her head. 'You're still under investigation for those CASA infringements, so I don't know if you want to mention to them that you just stole a helicopter to catch these guys, despite the justification.'

Nic nodded. 'So, this is a lesson for all of us. Just because it looks like a duck, sounds like a duck and most likely is a duck, it doesn't mean we should duck.'

Rose added. 'Well, at least we got to experience a little bit of the NT.'

Nic rubbed his hands together. 'Always look on the bright side of life. Let's wind things up, lock things down and head to the Airport. Another one dusted and busted for the good guys.'

The following morning, the group were sitting at the Airport bar about to go their separate ways. Kelleigh, Debacle and Elvis were returning to Perth, while Rose, Nic and Chewy were booked on a flight to Brisbane. Chewy opened his laptop and held out the palm of his hand toward Debacle. 'Can we at least see what she did? It was the cause of all of this.' Debacle sighed, took his cap off and carefully unwrapped the little parcel containing the chip. 'I hope it's enough.'

Elvis nodded. 'Me too.'

Chewy inserted the chip into an attachment linked to the computer and they watched the vision. The dialogue was clear and captured a heated argument regarding the previous CASA citations. It then showed Debacle and Aime wrestling for control of the helicopter, and eventually, she let go of the stick, saluted and dropped backwards from the helicopter into the water below. It was evident Debacle had done his best to maintain control. The vision continued: Debacle landed at Jandakot Airport and it showed him trying to remove the unit from the windscreen. Then it went black.

Chewy leaned back. 'You were lucky. The engine was still on when you removed the unit. It could've fried the chip and game over as evidence.'

Debacle sighed. 'I panicked. I remembered about that special needle thing but had no idea how to remove the dashcam from the windscreen. I hope I didn't damage it. Then about an hour later they turned up in the HiAce and they told me to help them load half the gold onto the plane. It was all so stupid. I should have ....I don't know.'

Nic put his hand on his shoulder. 'You strapped yourself to a winch and dangled from a helicopter doing about fifty kilometres an hour in the pursuit of a van full of gold. That accounts for something.' Debacle looked around at the others. 'I guess, but once the dust settles I need a big favour from all of you.' Elvis nodded. 'Another job? I'm sure we can work something out.' Debacle sighed. 'No, that's not it.....don't ever tell Connie what I did.'

Their flights were called and they said their goodbyes.

Heading due east towards Brisbane, and about two hours into their three-hour flight, Rose leaned over to Nic. 'What the latest with my Father's case? I have the diary, and as far as I know, John and Julia are safe from the clutches of Michael.'

Nic nodded. 'Well, we found Michael's crypto hardware wallet. It was shoved in the back of his old work computer. The Accountancy firm where he works, and they use that term loosely, had recently upgraded from tower boxes to laptops and Michael didn't retrieve the drive before they scrapped his old computer.'

'So, what's that got to do with my Father's diary.'

'You need both to access the crypto. The hardware wallet gives you the storage info, but the password is the key. It's a string of sixty-four numbers and letters. You don't keep the two together.'

Rose sighed. 'So, that's why were we playing computer Candy Crush, but the drive is about the size of a playing card. We didn't need to destroy everything.'

Nic shrugged. 'Recycling. On that final note, I'm going to catch some shut-eye.'

Rose looked at him. 'Oh no you don't. I have so many more questions.' Nic settled back into the chair; 'Please put them in writing,' and he was soon asleep.

Heading due west to Perth, Debacle leaned over to Elvis. 'What's the latest with mediation? Connie mentioned her Father is now involved.' Elvis nodded. 'It's been suspended until you return to face the music. I don't think it will have any traction after seeing that vision.'

Elvis then hesitated. 'You didn't tell me he's a Supreme Court Judge.' 'Nope, I didn't tell you lots of things about me. I'm not sure you want to know.' Elvis grinned. 'You can fly any helicopter, fly any plane and are prepared to hang on the end of a wire during the pursuit of a couple of dumb criminals. That's all I need to know. Having a judge in your back pocket is the icing on the cake, or gild on the gold, as the case may be.'

Debacle grimaced. 'He's my Father-in-Law, so not exactly in my back pocket.'

The plane landed and they were still sitting in the plane waiting to disembark when Kelleigh approached them and sat down in a seat opposite. 'Wow, remind me to ask Nic for an upgrade next time I work with him. Sitting in cattle class just doesn't seem to cut it when you two are up here, lounging in the pointy end.'

Debacle shrugged. 'What's up, Kelleigh?'

Kelleigh waved her phone. 'I just received a message. CASA has dropped their investigation. They decided there was no case to answer. You're free to keep flying.' Debacle sighed with relief. 'What about the flying in Alice Springs?'

'Well, about that. I had a word with the Arresting Sergeant, and as far as anyone knows Aime and Co. were caught before they tried to escape, not during, and certainly not flown back from somewhere near the MacDonnell Ranges dangling from a Chinook.'

Elvis grinned. 'So, he's finally off the hook?'

Kelleigh shook her head in dismay at his comment. 'You've been working with Nic far too long, and speaking of Nic, I'd better ring him and find out what I do about the elusive Nicolai Epine and Davit Poole.'

Debacle looked at her. 'You know that they are both Nic.'

Kelleigh nodded. 'Rose told me. Hopefully, they're still not looking for them.' Kelleigh dialled and Nic answered promptly, 'You're calling about the two missing men aren't you?'

'Yes, you must be psychic.'

'Yep, but I've got two sidekicks already, Rose and Chewy. I'm the man in the middle. Anyway, they've been taken care of as Chewy deleted their names from the ship's manifest.' Kelleigh sighed. 'I don't want to know how you've got access to that.'

'Well, if a bear scratches his backside against a tree in the woods and it falls over, the tree that is, not the bear. Was it ever there?'

'Goodbye Nic. I'd like to say it's been fun but......'

Nic waited for Kelleigh to continue but she had hung up.

25

Nic, Chewy and Rose arrived in Brisbane and drove directly to Nic's warehouse at Bowen Hills. The boxes of crushed computer bits were all gone and the place was very tidy. Rose looked around. 'Someone has been busy.'

'Yep, I have an army of elves that come in every day to make sure everything is tidy before you visit.'

'No, you don't. Elves only turn up at Christmas, Santa told me so.' Nic was about to respond when John and Julia exited from one of the offices. 'Thanks for the new gig, Nic. Hope we've tidied the space up to your liking.'

'Yep, thanks, Just send me the invoice.'

Rose approached them and they hugged. 'Have you spoken to my parents as yet?'

John nodded. 'We've come to an arrangement. We only work there part-time now, have three months off a year to go travelling, and can park the Winnebago on the tennis court.'

Rose smiled. 'Are you still living there?'

Julia nodded. 'Yes, we've hooked up to their water and power. Win-Win, I reckon.' Rose shrugged. 'Do you still have to cook for them?'

'Apparently not, Jana has discovered Door-Dash, so they order in. She hasn't told Zachariah yet, and he hasn't seemed to have noticed. He still can't work out where he left the diary though. He's getting a bit forgetful in his golden age.'

Rose nodded. 'Well, speaking of a golden age, thanks for all your help with the case. We made the right decision to leave to ship. It was all getting ugly. I got off in Adelaide and flew directly to Alice Springs. I didn't get a chance to catch up with Sandy.' Julia nodded. 'Is she still down there?'

'Yes, her Father hasn't fully recovered from COVID. I would say she's staying until he gets better. How long that takes, who knows.'

John sighed. 'Did you hear that Michael was attacked? Jana told me it was some kind of rabid animal, but there's no medical evidence to support that. Just a heap of scratches on his face and arms.'

Nic smiled. 'Attack of the Killer Cat. He tried to break into Rose's place looking for the diary. Got himself stuck in the cat-door and Dog did the rest.' John looked at him. 'He told Jana it was a bear.' Nic continued. 'The only bear we have in Australia is a drop-bear, it's part of the koala family. It is quite vicious apparently, although no one has ever seen one.'

Rose sighed. 'Michael is making it up, just like everything else he does. Did they mention anything more about the Crypto case?' John nodded. 'I heard there is a prelim hearing on Monday, I thought that's why you came back early from Alice Springs.'

Rose shook her head. 'No, the big end of town has taken over the gold thing now. Detective Kelleigh Brook has the case. She's based at Perth Police HQ but also has jurisdiction in the NT.' John continued. 'Michael's firm is denying any knowledge that such a crypto investment even exists as it's currently against their policy, so he has some explaining to do, but he's claiming a medical condition will prevent him from attending in person.'

Rose sighed again. 'And the court is happy with that?'

Julia shrugged. 'I saw the letter on the printer that he is presenting to them. It reads like it's written by a child. I was tempted to sign it "Yours Faithfully, Michael's Mum."

Nic nodded. 'So, we have until next week to put something together to minimise the impact on Zachariah, and shine the light on Michael.' Rose smiled. 'That will be interesting as he went to the same school of ethics as my Father, "Deny, deny, deny...and if not sure, blame someone else.'

John and Julia then headed off, and Rose headed home to West End stopping along the way to buy two hot roast chickens: one to reward Dog for guarding the house, and the other to share with her neighbour, Dave.

Nic, Rose and Chewy spent the next few days scouring through the myriad of files available on Michael's old computer. His firm had allowed Nic access to the hard drive to search for any incriminating evidence, and to deflect the blame from them, onto him if needed. The files mainly contained information relating to Michael's determination to get a promotion to Senior Partner. He had set up a folder for each of the existing partners which contained photographs, Word.doc notes and listings of any known associates. It was quite comprehensive. Nic was a little disappointed there wasn't a file on him.

Rose suddenly stopped. 'I've got something here you should look at.'

Nic smiled. 'Finally, as this is so boring. Please get me back out in the field.'

Chewy looked up. 'Hey, this is all I do, all day, every day. Data mining. It's not boring it's exciting. Only last week.....who am I kidding? I need a break too.'

Rose interrupted them. 'Did you want to see what I found?'

Nic nodded. 'Is it a link to funny cat videos? That's the only thing I watch.'

Rose shook her head. 'No, it appears to be a list of people and the amounts that Michael has diverted into cryptocurrency. There's about thirty names on it.'

Chewy looked over. 'I didn't see that file on the computer.'

Rose held up the diary. 'Old school. I was wondering why the front of the diary was thinner than the back. He'd stuck the pages together and I've managed to pry them apart.' Nic looked at Rose. 'Now, that is exciting. No wonder he's having conniptions trying to find it. Is there anyone on it that we know?'

'It's in code. Give me a second and I'll see if I can work out the key.' Rose re-read the first few names. 'I've got it.'

'That was quick. What is it?'

Rose grinned. 'The first name is his, but it reads: "Hsub Leahcim" It's just his name backwards. What a dope.'

Nic smiled. 'What about the numbers?'

'He's put the dollar sign at the end and used the symbols on the number keys.' Rose showed them the page and it read: "%)))$"

Nic looked at the keyboard and nodded. 'Five Thousand.'

Chewy shook his head at the simplicity of the code. 'I guess we would find the same list on the hard drive if we want to open the file.'

Nic shook his head. 'No point. We have the drive and his passwords. He can't access otherwise.' Rose smiled, then looked at Nic. 'I would love to see the look on his face when he finds out. Is he going to find out?'

Nic shrugged. 'I haven't worked out how we are going to play this one yet. I guess we go to the prelim hearing and see what's what.'

'OK, I'll give Mother a call and see if we can get invited.'

'No need. We've already been invited by Davide Reed, the Managing Partner at Michael's firm. He's appointed us to investigate the diversion of funds. Can you read out some of the other names to see if we know any of them.'

"Davad Tennet))))*$". Rose added 'That's a palindrome. Eight Thousand.'

"Noslen Edorf)))^!$". Nelson Forde – Sixteen Thousand.'

"Ris ghuh Nemrah))))%*$ ' Looks like Sir Hugh Harmen. Eighty five grand.'

Nic nodded. 'I think you can stop now. It's quite a bit of coin.'

'I'll just do one more. "**Dnumde Notrab))),)%@$. 'Edmund Barton. Two hundred and fifty thousand. I wonder what the double asterisk means.'

Nic hesitated. 'Did you say Edmund Barton?'

'Yes, why do you know him? Hang on, wasn't he out first Prime Minister?'

'He was, but he died in 1920. I don't think its him, but think I know why my Father is interested in this. It looks like Michael has somehow attracted some old money, and the top end of town might be getting a little anxious about it.'

Chewy opened his laptop browser. 'I'll check. I don't think there's an issue with politicians trading in crypto.' Chewy found a site he was looking for. 'It's not illegal, but they have to declare their interests, so having someone else holding it for you under an assumed name might just be.'

Nic sighed. 'I'd better contact my Father.'

Rose stood up and stretched. 'I thought you didn't have his number?'

'I don't. Give me a couple of minutes to set up the Bat-Signal.'

Rose shook her head. 'It's daylight. How is that going to work?'

'It's a digital signal.'

Nic stepped away and returned within a few minutes. 'He's already aware of it, but doesn't know how Michael got involved.'

Rose nodded. 'So what's next?'

'We put on our posh frocks and Sunday best and go along to the hearing on Monday to find out what's what.'

26

The prelim hearing was due to start at 11 o'clock. Nic, Chewy and Rose were waiting outside the Brisbane Courthouse in George Street to see who else would be arriving. A Rolls Royce stopped in the no-standing zone and Zachariah stepped out. Rose pointed the car out to the others. 'My Father is here, and it looks like he's alone. I wonder if Michael will come?'

Nic shook his head. 'I don't think so, he's got a letter from his mum.'

Chewy opened his phone and called Michael. 'Hello Sir, I believe you are to attend a hearing today for the missing cryptocurrency.' The call was immediately disconnected, and Chewy checked his phone locater app. 'It looks like he's at your parents place in Hamilton. I assume Zachariah couldn't convince him to attend.'

Zachariah had completely ignored them and made his way into the foyer, so Nic's group quickly followed him in. Rose approached him. 'Father.

Nice to see that you made it. Couldn't you convince Michael to attend?' He took a moment to realise it was Rose. 'I have no idea where Michael is. Why are you here?'

Rose sighed. 'Nic was appointed investigator on the case. So, I'm here as his associate along with Chewy.' Nic held out his hand. 'Nice to see you again, Mr Palmer.' Zachariah looked at Nic, then at his extended hand, and ignored it.

'This has nothing to do with you.'

Rose was about to reply when they saw Davide Reed enter the foyer. He approached them quickly. 'We're late. Follow me. Level 3. They changed the time by fifteen minutes.'

The group passed quickly through the security checkpoint and found their way to the conference room. Davide knocked on the door and they were ushered in. Two people were in the meeting - a judge and a stenographer were sitting at the head of the table, and a voice was coming through on the console unit in front of them. The judge leaned forward. 'Thank you for the update. I will be in touch after the outcome of this matter.' He then pressed the button to close the call then looked at the new arrivals.

'Please take a seat. You're late.'

Davide nodded. 'Apologies, Your Honour. We were only advised this morning of the change of time. I am Davide Reed, the Managing Partner at the Accountancy firm. This is Nic Thorn, my investigator and two of his associates.'

Davide then paused for Zachariah to introduce himself. They waited, but he said nothing.

The judge looked at a printout the stenographer had handed him. 'And you, sir?'

'Zachariah Emmerson Palmer. I have no idea why you are wasting my time.'

The judge ruffled the page. 'Well, Sir I believe you are implicated in a multi-million dollar cryptocurrency fraud. It is my time you are wasting not yours.' He looked at the stenographer. 'Don't worry about taking that note, Melinda. So, Zachariah Emmerson Palmer, are you any relation to Rose Palmer from the investigation team?' Zachariah ignored the question, so Rose responded. 'I am his daughter.'

The judge nodded. 'And Nic Thorn, are you any relation to Commander Thorn whom I have just been speaking to about this matter?'

'Yes, Sir. He is my Father.' Nic thought Chewy was about to make a comment about his family lineage, so quickly put his hand onto his arm. 'Not now, Chewy.'

The judge continued. 'My name is The Honourable Justice Hamilton Corey. I'm here to determine if there is sufficient evidence for the matter to proceed to trial. This is called a Settlement Conference. You are not under oath, nor have any obligation to tell the truth and you may request legal representation at any time. However, I have been doing this for quite some time and know when someone is being elusive, so do not try anything to make yourself look stupid.' The judge paused for effect. 'Now, I believe we are waiting on another person, a Mr Michael Bush. Does anyone know his whereabouts?'

Nic nodded. 'I believe he had advised the court he will not be attending, and has provided a letter to that effect.' The stenographer handed the judge a letter and the group assumed it was the one from Michael. He began to read it, then put it down onto the table. 'Can we confirm that it is written by Mr Bush?'

Nic nodded again. 'Yes, I have a copy. It was collected off a printer in Mr Palmers office after the letter was typed by Mr Bush on his laptop.' Zachariah glared at Rose. 'I did not give you permission to enter my office. How did you get it?' Rose sighed. 'We were given a copy in discovery and thought it would be worth keeping in case Michael doesn't turn up.'

Zachariah slammed his hand onto the table which caused Rose to jump. 'I will talk to you about that when I get home, Rosemary.'

The judge lightly strummed his fingers on the table. 'Now Mr Palmer, I think we have more matters to discuss rather than a copy of a letter. My question related to the validity of the letter and that has been answered to my satisfaction. Please explain to me your association with the cryptocurrency.'

Zachariah shook his head. 'I have no idea what you are talking about. I do not have access to cryptocurrencies, nor have any idea why I am even here. What sort of show are you running here?'

The judge sighed and clasped his fingers together. 'Do you deny that the account held in the name of Zachariah Palmer with the cryptocurrency company "Cashed-Up Investments" is yours?' Zachariah glared at him. 'Never heard of them.'

'Do you have an association with Michael Bush? Is he your Accountant? How well do you know him?' Zachariah grinned. 'He is my daughters ex-husband, and has been my Accountant for over ten years. I completely trust his judgement.'

Rose interjected. 'I was instructed to marry Mr Bush because of a deal my Father was trying to win. I was nineteen. The marriage lasted three days. It was annulled.' The stenographer stopped typing, took a breath, and waited for the next comment. Zachariah looked Rose. 'It's time you got over it, Rosemary.'

The judge sighed again. 'Please delete those last two comments, Melinda. They are not relevant to this case. Does anyone else have anything to say?'

Nic nodded. 'Yes, Your Honour. We located the Hardware Wallet and also have in our possession a diary containing the password key. We believe we have also uncovered a list of names along with the amount of said investments held under the sole name of Zachariah Palmer and would like to hand it to the court as evidence.' Nic held up the small black box, diary and a printout of the names.

The judge took a moment to understand the significance of Nic's statement. 'How did they come to be in your possession?'

Davide replied instead. 'The hardware unit was located during the search of superseded computer equipment owned by my office. I believe the diary was inadvertently collected by Mr Palmer's housekeeper when she was boxing up some of her own books.' Zachariah looked sternly at the judge. 'Michael wants the diary back. I demand you give it to him.' The judge stood up, ignored his request and took possession of the two items. 'Please tell Mr Bush to make an appointment with me and I will consider handing them over. I believe I have heard enough today, and will adjourn this hearing until such time that Mr Bush sees fit to explain to me what is going on. You are all free to leave.'

Nic's group, along with Davide Reed began to leave however Zachariah remained seated. 'Corey. Explain to me why I am here?' The judge looked at him. 'I would appreciate that you call me "Your Honour," I think I've earned it.'

'Well, *Your Honour*, why am I here? I have already told you I don't know anything about the cryptocurrency. I have no association with that company, and have no idea how it came to be. You cannot detain me.'

The judge sighed. 'I'll explain it layman's terms. I believe that Mr Michael Bush has been investing in Bitcoin without authorisation from his Accountancy Firm and the account is in your name. Furthermore, I now have in my possession access to the account. I will hold these until such time we meet again.' The judge looked at Nic. 'I will give you forty eight hours to locate Mr Bush and present him to me. Until then, please leave Mr Palmer before I hold you in contempt and throw you back in jail.'

Rose gasped, but Nic grinned as he knew the judge was bluffing as his jurisdiction in the Settlement Hearing would not extend to such an order. The judge continued. 'Rose, please assist your Father to leave this office.'

Zachariah stood up and huffed. 'I'm going. I don't need your help, Rosemary.'

27

A little time later, Nic, Rose and Chewy had returned to the warehouse at Bowen Hills. Zachariah had been collected by his driver, and Davide Reed had headed off to his office. Rose sighed. 'That was getting very ….tense. We have to find Michael ASAP.'

Chewy nodded. 'He was at your folks place, but it looks like he's moved on.'

'How do you know that?'

'We've got trackers on him.'

'Do you mean his phone? That's not much good, he could lose it.'

Chewy smiled. 'Not quite, I left a GPS tracker with John and he has put it on Michael's car.' Nic nodded. 'He's likely to do the round of three places: Home at Brookwater, at Browns Plains or at Hamilton. I don't think he'll go to his office.'

Rose nodded. 'I agree. He doesn't have any friends, so there's no need to check out anywhere else. So, do we split up and try find him?'

'Yep. I'll get Chewy to go to Browns Plains. I'll go to Brookwater and drop you off at your folks place along the way. I'm sure your Father would like to see you.' Rose grimaced 'I think I'd rather spend the time with them rather that Dimond.'

Nic drove to Hamiton and helped Rose from the car. 'Keep safe and call me if he turns up.' Rose nodded. 'I will, but I'm not sure how my Father will take me being here. I spoke to Julia this morning and they're spending the day on the Gold Coast. I'll be on my own.' Rose sighed, closed the car door and Nic drove away.

Rose looked up at the sprawling mansion where she grew up. 'This place used to be so....' But she didn't get to complete the sentence as a hand clamp firmly on her shoulder. It was Michael. 'You're coming with me.' He then took her arm and bent it behind her back. 'Ow, that hurts. What do you want, Michael?'

'The diary, the hardware unit and the reason why you stuck your stupid nose into my stupid business.' Rose tried to wriggle out of his grasp but he applied more pressure. 'It's fraud and illegal, Michael. You can't invest other people's money into Bitcoin. What made you think it was a good idea?' Michael barked at her. 'Shut up, and get in.' He pushed her towards a white van parked on the street, and Rose realised it wasn't the beige Camry that he usually drives.

He used the remote to unlock the rear doors and pushed her inside. 'You're going for a ride and give me your phone.'

Rose handed over her phone, then Michael dropped it to the ground and stomped on it. 'Nic is not going to save you this time.' Michael then stepped into the driver's seat and drove along the road.

Rose sat down and hung on. 'What about Dimond and the girls? Surely they don't want to see you doing this. This is kidnapping.'

Michael barked again. 'Shut up, Rose. Dimond is picking up the girls from school and taking them home for the weekend. She'd been spending time here looking after your Mother and Father, which is a lot more that you've done.'

Rose rode out the latest bump. 'My parents can handle themselves. They have to now that John and Julia won't be around as much. Julia gave us the diary, and now it's in the hands of the judge. I worked out your stupid name and numbers code too. You're such a dope.'

Michael called back. 'I'm the dope? You're the one sitting in the back of the van rolling around like a piece of trash.' Michael swung the steering wheel from side to side which caused Rose to slide across the floor and slam into other side.

'You're really annoying me now, Michael.'

EIGHT DAVE'S ARE WEAK - 255

Nic soon arrived at Brookwater and pulled his car to a stop. There was a beige Camry parked in the driveway, so he jogged up to it and looked inside. There were two small suitcases on the back seat along with shredded pink birthday wrapping paper. Nic went to the door. rung the bell and one of the girls opened it. She looked at him. 'You're not a clown. Daddy said there would be a clown.' The young girl began to wail. 'Mummy, there's a man at the door. He's not dressed as a clown. You promised.'

A few moments later Dimond came to the door. 'Hello Nic. Thanks for coming to Skye's birthday party. You're the first to arrive.' Nic looked at her. 'I'm not here for the party. I'm looking for Michael. He was supposed to be in court this morning.'

Dimond smiled. 'I know, he told me all about it. He's been in Brisbane all this time. Told me he'd been staying at a friend's place at Bowen Hills. I was surprised at that as I didn't know he had any friends.'

Nic sighed. 'Where is he, Dimond?'

'I left him at Rose's parents place. He said he had things to do. I picked up the girls and drove home. He's been driving a rental and not even anything special, just a stupid white van with "Wrent a Wreck" on it.' Dimond nodded to her car. 'I hate driving that beige car. It's as boring as he is.'

Nic shook his head. 'That's not good.'

Nic stepped away and called Chewy. 'He's still at Hamilton.'

Chewy responded. 'No, he's at Brookwater.' Nic hesitated. 'His car is a Brookwater. Check the phone tracker.'

Chewy came back a moment later 'It's at Brookwater too. Crap, I only put a tracker on his phone, he's probably still using the burner. Meet me at Hamilton ASAP.'

Nic closed the call, jumped back into his car and drove off. Dimond watched him go and Skye looked up at her. 'Is Daddy coming to the party dressed as a clown?'

Dimond sighed. 'He doesn't need to dress up.'

Nic and Chewy arrived at Hamilton roughly at the same time. Nic leaped over the front fence, scaled the stairs three at a time and banged his fist on the front door. 'Open up, it's Nic Thorn. Michael has kidnapped Rose.' Zachariah and Jana came to the door. 'Calm down, Mr Thorn. What's this all about?' Nic responded quickly. 'We know Michael was here instead of being at the hearing and we believe he has kidnapped Rose.'

Jana added. 'He told me he didn't need to go, and why would he take Rose? He just wants the diary back. He wouldn't hurt her. He thinks he's still in love with her.'

Nic looked at Jana. 'It's been over ten years. It's time he got over it. He's been re-directing funds from his clients and investing it in Bitcoin under Zachariah's name. That's why your husband was arrested.' Zachariah looked at him. 'Why would he do that?'

Chewy joined them on the front porch. 'To make money. The value of Bitcoin has gone up many thousands of dollars. He's put it in, then will cash it out and keep the difference. He's been lucky that it hasn't tanked.'

Jana looked at him. 'Why doesn't everybody do that if it is such a good investment?'

Nic shook his head. 'It's too volatile, but I'm not going to stand here and discuss the ins and outs of crypto. Where do you think Michael would've taken Rose?' Jana shook her head. 'We have no idea?'

'Think, Damn it We all know he doesn't have any friends, he's not at Brookwater or Browns Plains. Where else does he .....' Nic stopped talking. 'I've just had a thought. Chewy, get back to the car. We'll try the XXX Strip Club at Spring Hill.' Jana watched them scramble down the stairs. 'I'll open the gate for you.' Nic called back. 'Don't bother', and they both hurdled the metre high English box hedge. Jana looked at Zachariah. 'I think we need to have a word to Mr Croud about raising the height of our front fence.'

Michael drove the van down a narrow laneway and parked it at the rear of the building. Rose stood up and recognised where they were via the view through the front windscreen. 'You still come to this place? Does Dimond know?'

'Shut up, Rose. I'm thinking.' Michael then made a phone call.

Rose sat down and tipped the content of her handbag onto the floor of the van. *'There must be something I can use as a weapon.'* Rose discarded various objects and considered whether spraying him with her perfume might work. She was deciding on the nail clippers when she noticed she still had the earbud she'd used on the cruise ship, so placed it inside her ear. There was no sound. Nothing.

Michael then stepped out of the van and moved along side, opened the rear doors and beckoned Rose to come out. 'No. I'm not getting out, Michael.'

'Oh, yes you are.' Michael climbed in and grabbed her by the arm. 'You're coming inside with me as there's someone I'd like you to meet.'

Rose opened her hand, looked at the nail clippers and decided they wouldn't be of any use, so she kicked her bottle of Chanel No. 5 out the door and deliberately stomped on it as she stepped out. Michael looked at the broken shards of glass.

'What did you do that for? I'm going to have to buy you another one now.'

'I got it for Valentines Day.'

'Michael grinned. 'I know.'

Nic and Chewy had made the normally fifteen minute drive from Hamilton to Spring Hill in under ten minutes. Nic slowed down when he arrived on Upper Edward Street, then did a left hand turn into a laneway running alongside the XXX building. He pulled the car to a stop in the carpark but there wasn't a white van in it. 'Damn it, Rose. Where are you?'

Chewy stepped out of the car. 'Can you smell that?'

'What?'

'Perfume. It's ....strong. How can I smell that at two in the afternoon?' Nic shrugged. 'Maybe there's a back entrance to the venue or something?' Chewy nodded. 'It's not back here. The rear entrance door is on the side.'

Nic took another sniff. 'The perfume...it smells like Chanel. Rose sometimes wears it. I was going to buy Rose and Sandy a bottle each for Valentines Day, but Rose said she already received one. I sent Rose Lisianthus instead, and Sandy a bouquet of roses. Anonymously of course.'

They began searching for the origin of the fragrance and located the glass shards on the ground.

'Maybe she was here?' Nic took a moment to consider what to do next, then looked at his watch. 'Do you think she still has the earbud?'

Chewy shrugged. 'I thought you took it off her?'

Nic shook his head. 'Nup, I tried. She thought I was about to kiss her on the cheek, so she kept it.' Nic turned the function on, increased the intensity to full volume and they watched the watch and waited.

Inside the building, Michael led Rose through the myriad of darkened rooms and dumped her into a seat inside a curtained booth. 'Stay here.' Rose shrugged and closed her eyes 'I'm not going anywhere until you tell me what's going on.'

'Shut up.'

Rose was about to respond when the earbud began to buzz. 'I think you're in trouble now, Michael.'

'Shut up. No one knows we're here.'

Rose raised her voice and responded. 'Where else would you be? Chewy went to your hidey-hole at Browns Plains and Nic went to your house at Brookwater. You don't have many places to go or any friends to help you out of this mess.'

Michael stepped back through the curtain and Rose could overhear him talking to someone, so called out 'Help...he's kidnapped me.' The curtains opened and the silhouette of a man appeared among the shroud. 'Sounds like fun, little lady.'

Rose stood up. 'Can you please turn off the earbud it's giving me a headache.'

Nic, Chewy and Rose were waiting outside the front of the XXX club for the Police to arrive. Rose had found a lovely pair of pink fluffy handcuffs for Michael to wear and he was sitting down on the kerb.

Rose smiled. 'You found the van then?'

Nic shook his head. 'No, it was the perfume, Chanel No. 5 I believe. A pleasant floral bouquet composed around rose and jasmine and elevated by aldehydes.'

Michael looked up. 'Yes, and cost me over four hundred dollars. Next time I'm sending flowers.'
Rose grinned 'Well, don't send Lisianthus. I already get a bunch of them. Anonymously of course.'

Nic shrugged, then added. 'What happened to the van, Michael?'

Michael sighed. 'It got stolen. I left the keys in it when I was taking Rose inside. You can't trust anyone these days. The rental people rang me as it was used in a hit and run. I'm up for the full damages.'

Nic nodded. 'Crime doesn't pay, Michael. You know you'll do jail time and probably lose your job.' Michael shrugged. 'What's the big deal? So I invested in crypto? I made some people a lot of money. I wasn't going to keep it all for myself.'
Rose shook her head. 'Stop talking Michael.'

The police arrived and Michael was led to the Paddy Wagon. Nic was about to close the door when he realised he needed to know about one of the names on the list. 'Who was Edmund Barton to you and why the asterisks?'

Michael smiled. 'He was the first Prime Minister of Australia.'

Nic shook his head. 'Is there a connection to another person?'

'No, it's just me. My Father always told me I was good enough to be the Prime Minister one day if I truly believe it.'

Rose shook her head. 'You're an idiot, Michael.'

Nic stepped away. 'I need to make a call.'

Rose watched him go. 'He's calling his Father isn't he?' Chewy nodded. 'I would suspect so. We almost got to meet him didn't we.'

Rose smiled. 'Haven't you met him either? I thought you two were cousins?'

Chewy shrugged. 'I've never met him or seen him. Maybe one day.'

Nic returned and had overhead their conversation, so he added. 'And I don't know what he sounds like either.'

Introducing Book 9 in the Nic Thorn & Associates series: Nine Means Nothing.

Rosemary Palmer was surrounded by darkness, but it wasn't the darkness you seek while trying to get to sleep under a warm woollen doona, it was the darkness of a moonless night somewhere north of the middle of nowhere. Rose, however, wasn't exactly nowhere, as she was located nine kilometres southwest of Charters Towers, a semi-rural town located in Far North Queensland.

Rose checked the time on her phone: 4.19 a.m., exhaled and watched her warm breath float away into the early morning mist. 'Damn you, Nic. It's the middle of July, and not supposed to be this cold in the tropics.'

A voice responded in her earbud. 'Tell me about it, spud.' It was her friend, mentor and scam busting associate, Nic Thorn. 'Rose, if nothing happens now, we'll try again tomorrow night. You can keep watch from the back instead of the front.'

Rose mouthed a silent scream and raised her infrared night vision binoculars to focus on the front window of the nearby property. 'There has to be something here. Show me something.' There was nothing, and her teeth continued to chatter with the cold. 'Double damn you, Nic, Nic.'

Somewhere not so far away, Sandy Fraser, the third wheel in the trio's scams, frauds and genuine misunderstandings investigative team, sipped on her fourth coffee and thumbed the remote on the heater pushing it closer to Maximum. It was a tough gig, but someone had to stay awake at the Airbnb to keep the home fires burning and the coffee perking.

Sandy picked up the two-way radio. 'This is Ranger Smith. Are you on channel Yogi and Boo-Boo?'

Nic tapped his ear. 'Yep, but I thought I was Ranger Smith?'

A response came from Rose. 'That makes me either Yogi or Boo-Boo. I don't think I'm either. I need a hot shower and a hot coffee, not necessarily in that order.' Nic responded softly. 'Another hour, Rose. It gets light soon.'

'Triple damn you, Nic, Nic, Nic.'

Sandy pulled a rug around her shoulders and shuffled closer to the warmth emanating from the heater. 'How about I take your shift tomorrow night. It's too cosy in here anyway.'

'Thanks, I owe you one...' Rose was about to add something else when she suddenly noticed some movement. 'This is Boo-Boo, Yogi...damn it, it's me. I think there's something moving by the house.' Nic responded. 'Which side?'

'The underside, the left hand side. It's ...nope it's gone.'

Nic slowly raised himself up from his hidey-hole and brushed himself down. 'I'm going in for a closer look. Call me if you see anything or anyone come out.' He edged his way toward the property and pressed himself up against a small, corrugated iron shed. 'I can't see anything from here. I'm going closer.'

Rose whispered. 'Be careful. It might be a drop-bear.'

Nic pressed his earbud. 'Did it have one or two little black beady eyes?'

'No idea, but what difference does that make? It might have been winking at me.'

For more reading from the Nic Thorn and Associates Series of scam-busting capers, try the first novel 'One Tricked Phoney' where it all began:

One Tricked Phoney

Rose needed a +1, but not for the usual wedding/party. She was going to a funeral and needed a quiet, unassuming type. The best option was to use her dating site, but when Nic Thorn arrived, he was anything but a wallflower. This very first adventure leads them from one lively caper to another, this time involving portrait provenance, invoice inaccuracy, and a recycler's relapse, on their travels from Brisbane, Adelaide, to the SA border.

Two hurtled Gloves

Rose Palmer was to be a bride again, but this time, Nic Thorn ensured it wasn't the short, fat and shallow man her parents forced her to marry the first time. Together with her BFF Sandy, they move onto another tale, this one tracking down the elusive and believed to be extinct Thylacine. Sandy loses her identity, and they get introduced to the benign world of banking, but there is much more involved when the loan arranger is unmasked as a fraud.

Three French Bens

Nic's friend, Benoit Trudeau, is one-third of the 'Three French Bens'. He has just bought into a high-end restaurant, so he called Nic's Team in to have a look, as the numbers look fishy, and they might have to go angling for the truth. Nic and his crew then head to Rockhampton to help the Queensland Department of Agriculture inspect some cattle duffing and Sandy has to deal with an old school friend, or is that a fiend lending to her at her expense?

Four brooding Birds

The Australian Department of Agriculture often deals with sneaks and adders, and this time, Nic and the team are brought in to investigate reptile smuggling. Lizards have been discovered stuffed into a women's singlet, and her accomplice is caught with his own jocks of frogs, but they deny any knowledge of how they got in there. Then the team tries to drink from the sweet success of wines, but it turns out to be someone who can't stop whining about how he has to keep everything bottled up inside and to complete their investigation they have to look into genuine budgie smugglers.

Five Mouldy Bins

It's Christmas in July, and the Department of Health in Brisbane is concerned that someone may be stuffing their mattress with ill-gotten gains, so Nic and the team are brought in to bring it to a head – reindeer style. Sandy and Rose meet up with their 'friend' Dimond, who keeps handing over her hard-earned money to lease a new rental property for her husband and family as it turns out the Real Estate Agent knows how to manage to take the deposit too, but only ever in cash. Then, the team gets involved in a diamond scam. The resolution could be clear cut, but getting stranded in Dubai on the way to South Africa was never in the plan.

Six Geezers Lying

Car insurance companies are driven up the wall by bogus claims and 'accidents' and it's about time someone gives the scammers a crash course on how to stop. Then, one of the national restaurant chains puts together a competition so easy that anyone can win, but what happens when the prizes are won before the contest is finished? The team then gets involved in an art scam, and Rose's Father is in the middle of it. Art is not always art but scamming is always fraud.

Seven Hapless Hoops

This time they head to Ouyen, Nic's home town, on the Victorian and South Australian border. Not everyone likes a homecoming, especially if you like to keep secrets, and people need to know their superheroes come in all shapes and sizes- not just flashy capes and disguises. Meantime a car vanishes without a trace in Mildura, Victoria, and everyone knows that making an elephant disappear is done with smoke and mirrors, but in this case it's a car worth over seven hundred thousand dollars. Then, a dog and pony show gathers pace on Kangaroo Island, off the coast of South Australia.

Author's Biography:

The author is a former long-term banker by profession and worked in the Bank's Credit Card Fraud Team, where he obtained a Private Investigators Licence. The author resides between Adelaide, South Australia, and the Sunshine Coast, Queensland.

In November 2022, the author won an award from Wakefield Press, Adelaide for his short story: 'Car on a Hill'.

The following Nic Thorn and Associates titles are available for online purchase; e-Book or paperback, or direct from the author: One Tricked Phoney, Two Hurtled Gloves, Three French Bens, Four Brooding Birds, Five Mouldy Bins, Six Geezers Lying, Seven Hapless Hoops and Eight Dave's are Weak. To be published in 2026: Nine Means Nothing and Ten Little Idioms.

Other titles written by the author:
Driven to Kill.
The Flighters – Believe.

www.ingramcontent.com/pod-product-compliance
Lightning Source LLC
Chambersburg PA
CBHW071233070526
44583CB00017B/2158